#215

Checklist Management:

The Eight-Hour Manager

© **Jeffrey P. Davidson** 1986

A Plain English Press Book
National Press, Inc.
7508 Wisconsin Avenue
Bethesda, Maryland 20814
(301) 657-1616

Library of Congress Cataloging-in-Publication Data

Davidson, Jeffrey P.
    Checklist management.

    Bibliography: p.
    1. Management. 2. Personnel management.
3. Supervision of employees. I. Title.
HD31.D245 1986   658.3   86-5377
ISBN 0-915765-26-8

DEDICATION

This book is dedicated with love, to Shirley Davidson who, especially in the last nine years, really showed her stuff, and to Eileen Kelley, who took life's toughest punches but always came up smiling.

ACKNOWLEDGMENT

I would like to acknowledge the creative talent and input provided by Richard Davidson whose assistance was instrumental in the development of Chapter 18, Handling the Data Processing Professional; Chapter 21, Working with the Underachiever; Chapter 28, Playing Would-Be Lou Grant; and Chapter 42, Honing Your Professional Skills. Dianne Walbrecker put Chapters 34 to 36 in excellent form. Nancy Davidson merits recognition for her expertise in the development of Chapter 37, Helping the Battered Employee. Shirley Davidson helped formulate the concept for Chapter 19, Improving the Quality of Interruptions. Don Long's research on absenteeism was essential. Rose Bravo ably edited and typed the entire manuscript in her usual highly professional manner. Finally, I would like to thank my publisher, Joel Joseph, for his numerous editorial contributions, marketing capabilities, and consistently high level of enthusiasm.

CONTENTS

CHARTS, DIAGRAMS

CHECKLISTS

SECTION I

STARTING OFF RIGHT

Congratulations! You're now a manager. Whether you recently assumed this role, or have had it for a while you've quickly learned that every working day your staff counts on you for direction, feedback, support and leadership. Any way you look at it, it's a large, potentially high-stress, seemingly never-ending task. And, to further complicate matters, your organization, department or division asks more and more of you as you begin to have less time.

A major 14 year ongoing study conducted by Arthur D. Little, which examined 250,000 employees at over 200 companies indicates a decline in confidence among employees regarding their organization's top management, middle management and direct supervisors. The study *Supervision in the 1980s: Trends in Corporate America,* by Brian S. Morgan, Ph.D. and William A. Schiemann, Ph.D. indicates that in many organizations the amount of communication from the top is severely restricted and that the failure to share this information with workers leaves a void of uncertainty. Moreover, American business faces a new kind of transient worker "uncertain of the future, cynical about getting ahead, susceptible to union blandishments and determined to look for more stable environs. While the grass may not be greener elsewhere it often appears to be." Morgan and Schiemann point out that only 21% of clerical employees currently feel that they are being treated fairly, and less than 5% of clerical and other hourly workers rate their companies as among the best or above average—a sharp downturn from the 1970s. They also point to a crisis of confidence in corporate leadership today which extends *all the way down to the level of immediate supervisor.* For every story and blockbuster book we see on the resurgence of American business enterprise, there are hundreds of thousands of line workers that don't feel any better about their jobs or their company, and indeed may feel a whole lot worse. "Stress" and "burnout" have become synonymous with the 80's. There's not a one minute technique in the world that will give managers a handle on the vast array of daily problems they face.

Against this backdrop, what can managers and supervisors do to assemble or develop a winning team that accomplishes assigned goals and objectives while working in unison and remaining friendly?

Read on!

In this first section "Starting Off Right" which encompasses Chapters 1 through 8, we'll discuss how to assemble or develop an effective staff that can help to make both your job and theirs more enjoyable.

CHAPTER ONE
SO, YOU'RE THE BOSS

The terms supervisor and manager are often used interchangeably. Perhaps the best description of the role of the supervisor is offered in William S. Dinsmor's classic article in the July 1962 issue of *Personnel Magazine*. Dinsmor, then a general partner of management, human resources and compensation specialists, Edward N. Hay and Associates, pointed out that the basic distinction between supervision and management is that "supervision involves overseeing one generally cohesive function, whereas management involves integrating and coordinating dissimilar functions that are related in having a common objective." More precisely, a supervisor is one who tells people what to do and how to do it.

The supervisor directly oversees the work of one or more individual employees while also maintaining many of his/her own operating duties—all in the connection with the performance of a single cohesive function. The manager is one "who tells people in fairly specific terms what to accomplish and then counsels them to the extent necessary in their efforts to accomplish these objectives." The manager integrates and coordinates numerous dissimilar functions which all contribute to the same goal or set of goals.

The information and recommendations presented in this book relate to both supervisors and managers.

What makes an effective manager/supervisor? Well, the list is endless. And the answer can be as diverse as the number of business executives and authors alive today. Here's a checklist of some key items:

CHART 1

THE SUCCESSFUL MANAGER

Characteristics
- ☐ Shows **flexibility** in handling situations
- ☐ Readily assumes **responsibility**
- ☐ Maintains an **even keel** even during emergencies
- ☐ Is **energetic** and generally in good health
- ☐ Is **receptive** to different approaches and opinions of others
- ☐ **Adapts** to new situations or accepts change
- ☐ Maintains **productivity** even under poor conditions
- ☐ Effectively **juggles** many tasks at the same time
- ☐ Maintains proper **perspective** in approach to problems and handling staff

Approach
- ☐ Accepts calculated **risk**
- ☐ Examines problems from **many angles**
- ☐ Identifies **crucial elements** of large tasks
- ☐ Avoids getting bogged down by **details**
- ☐ Incorporates **new information** and data quickly
- ☐ Avoids management by crisis by **troubleshooting** and preventative measures
- ☐ Incorporates **changes in technology** or methods that will improve operations

Communication
- ☐ **Motivates** staff to do their best
- ☐ **Anticipates** reaction of others to new ideas and suggestions
- ☐ Develops effective **listening** capability
- ☐ Seeks **cooperation**with other departments/divisions
- ☐ Maintains **open channel** with upper management
- ☐ Allocates sufficient **time for planning**
- ☐ Offers effective **day-to-day** coordination
- ☐ **Matches staff capabilities** with appropriate tasks
- ☐ Makes decisions with **confidence**

Whew! Perhaps no one has ever completely mastered all the points listed in Chart One. Nevertheless, the chart is useful as a guide or a model for which to strive.

All for You

The content and format of this chapter, as in all other chapters in this book, have been especially prepared for you, the modern manager. Numerous checklists are offered which can be readily photocopied and applied as needed. Long-winded passages dwelling on supervisory theory have been virtually eliminated and replaced with quick, easy-to-digest information that you can apply immediately.

Chances are you will read through the whole book only once, but will need to refer to specific sections over and over again. To accommodate this need, chapters have been sliced up into convenient, "digestible" portions.

In addition, the text has been adorned with numerous captioned illustrations, many of an amusing nature, to help reinforce and highlight the suggestions offered. Let's turn now to Chapter Two, Identifying and Attracting Talent, to learn how an effective team can be assembled.

CHAPTER TWO

IDENTIFYING AND ATTRACTING TALENT

One of the most important factors in the long term success of an organization is hiring the right people to begin with. There is no substitute for good employees, and while the supervisor's job will always require a multitude of activities, having the right people on board can enable one to have more time to devote to other areas. Regardless of the size of the organization for which you work, chances are you have some responsibility for identifying and attracting effective staff members.

This chapter will help you to answer these questions:

□ What is a **job description** and how is it used?
□ What are the **key components** of a job description?
□ What items are contained on a **good application form**?
□ Why should the effective supervisor always keep an eye out for **new talent**?
□ What are some sources for **attracting new talent**?
□ Why and how are **blind box advertisements** used?

Job Descriptions

Tom Hanlon was recently promoted to supervisor in the Northwest sales office of a durable goods manufacturing company. Tom hadn't even been at the new position for two weeks when he received a memo indicating that his assistance was requested in developing a job description for the new staff position that had been created. It suddenly occurred to Tom that although he knew the operations of the department inside and out, he had never actually written a job description and was reluctant to admit to anyone that this was the case.

16

THE JOB MARKET

You might be asked to prepare a job description. The purpose of defining a job prior to recruiting is that it clarifies the type of person wanted, and also assists in writing classified advertisements or other copy to attract qualified job candidates.

The job description should include specific duties, and working conditions, and working relationships the employee will encounter. It should clearly identify the qualifications and skills, including education and experience, that prospective employees must have, as well as the behavior expected on the job. It is also advisable to include personal characteristics that are desired and will be an aid to job performance (e.g., promptness, physical strength, desire for increased responsibilities). After the job description is written it should be circulated to the personnel office or to the supervisor's boss to determine if the description is appropriate. (See examples, next page.)

Although the job description should leave no doubt in an applicant's mind about the qualification for the job, it is important to remain flexible about job specifications. Remember, the "ideal" employee exists only in one's mind. By being too demanding, you may cause your organization to end up paying higher salaries or having to wait much longer for positions to be filled.

Larry G. McDougle of Indiana University at Kokomo points out that many organizations operate with either inadequate job descriptions or none at all. But a well-constructed job description simplifies performance appraisals, helps prevent supervisors from making judgments based on inadequate measurements and even helps orient new workers.

Here's his list of key components of a superior job description:

- ☐ Position, title and classification.
- ☐ Description of proposed duties and responsibilities. (Might include activities organized according to frequency.)
- ☐ List of skills and special knowledge necessary.
- ☐ Outline of working conditions, especially any that are out of the ordinary.
- ☐ Description of the type of supervision that the position requires and who gives it. Also, to what extent there is supervision of others.
- ☐ Qualifications: Education and work experience.
- ☐ Full or part-time. Permanent or temporary.
- ☐ Salary grades. Allowances.
- ☐ Nature of contact with other groups, such as the general public, other departments or government officials.
- ☐ Type of personal judgment, initiative or resourcefulness required.

Job Description (blank)

POSITION, TITLE, CLASSIFICATION _____

_____

LOCATION _____
DESCRIPTION OF DUTIES _____

_____

WHY THIS OPENING HAS OCCURRED _____

_____

AUTHORITY & LIMITATIONS _____

_____

WHO/WHAT THE JOB WILL EFFECT
(i.e. geography, department, market)

_____

SUPPORT STAFF, RESOURCES _____

_____

REPORTS TO _____
MINIMUM QUALIFICATIONS _____

_____

HOURS _____

_____

EMPLOYMENT OPPORTUNITY
Department of Transportation
Equipment Management, Heavy Equipment Section
1283 Seven Locks Road, Rockville, MD

Department of Liquor Control
Division of Wholesale Operations, Warehouse Section
1665 Crabbs Branch Way, Rockville, MD

Announcement No: 098400C

WE ARE ACCEPTING APPLICATIONS FOR THIS POSITION ON AN OPEN AND CONTINUOUS BASIS

THIS POSITION IS BEING ADVERTISED TO ESTABLISH AN ELIGIBLE LIST FOR CURRENT AND FUTURE VACANCIES

The Montgomery County Departments of Transportation and Liquor Control are seeking applicants for the position of Mechanic II. The employee will be responsible for skilled mechanical work at the journeyman level in the maintenance and repair of complex automotive, material-handling and construction equipment, such as gasoline and diesel motors, buses, tractors, bulldozers, graders, forklifts, conveyor systems and other county equipment. Employee will work on of the following shifts to be assigned as needed: 7:30 a.m.–4:00 p.m.; 3:30 p.m.–12:00 midnight; or 11:30 p.m.–8:00 a.m.

CHART2C

JOB DESCRIPTION

POSITIONS AVAILABLE

WHO/WHAT THE JOB WILL EFFECT

SUPPORT STAFF, RESOURCES

RECOMMENDED QUALIFICATIONS

SALARY

POSITION LOCATION

DESCRIPTION OF DUTIES

MINIMUM QUALIFICATIONS

HOURS

POSITION: **EXPORT SALES MANAGER, MIDDLE EAST**

DUTIES: Promotion of our products in the Middle East. Follow up on all enquiries. Direct clerical staff in expediting export correspondence, bid requests, credit collections. Supervise shipping details, export licenses, customs declarations. Arrange preparation of foreign language technical manuals. Provide technical and consultant assistance and public relations. Supervise on-site equipment installation. Provide inventory of spare parts for local service stations. Maintain current information on import-export tariffs, licenses and restrictions. Supervise duties of a secretary and an expeditor.

REQUIREMENTS: Minimum five years experience in audio visual, special effects, animation, film lab and/or related electronic systems, or
Previous experience in sales of Oxberry or related equipment overseas.
Knowledge of Middle East language is highly recommended (Arabic, Farsi and/or Turkish)
Travel to the territories of the Middle East

HOURS: Full-time flexible

SALARY: $26,000 per year
Report or send resume to **N.J. Job Service, Henry Street, Passaic, N.J. 00000. (201) 070-1200 Ref. J.O. #0900080 No fee charged.**

Note: This description might also have included: who to report to; why this opening has occurred; position authority and limitations.

The Application Blank

Undoubtedly your organization uses some type of job application blank. The application blank is one of the many tools the middle manager uses in evaluating job candidates. A good application form should at a minimum request the following information:

- ☐ Identifying information, such as name, address, telephone number, and social security number.
- ☐ Physical characteristics, such as height, weight, and health, and physical limitations.
- ☐ Education, including specialized training, courses or seminars.
- ☐ Experience through at least the last three or four employers.
- ☐ References, at least three; more is better.
- ☐ Other interests, clubs, associations, community involvement.

In determining what information is to be collected on an application blank, it is necessary to reach a middle ground between the information that is desired and needed, and what can be obtained effectively on a two to three page form. (see sample Chart 3)

The application blank should not be used as the sole basis for hiring decisions. It's main usefulness is to provide information for checking references and to facilitate good interviewing.

Talent Sources

In addition to newspaper advertisements, there are many other sources that can be considered when identifying qualified personnel:

- ☐ Recommendations of present employees
- ☐ State and local job banks
- ☐ Professional and trade associations
- ☐ College placement offices
- ☐ Employment agencies
- ☐ Previous employees
- ☐ Customers and suppliers
- ☐ Competitors employees

Resume exchanges with other departments and non competing organizations, depending on the nature of the work to be done, and the following sources, should not be overlooked:

☐ Mental health organizations.
☐ Vocational clinics.
☐ Trade and technical schools.
☐ Handicapped worker's associations.

When seeking qualified part-time help, all of the above sources should be considered, as well as the following:

☐ Association of Part-time Professionals, Washington, DC
☐ American Association of Retired Persons, Washington, DC
☐ Summer internships for students through local colleges.
☐ Student work-study programs through local high schools.
☐ Temporary employment agencies which may prove to be far less expensive than adding permanent employees.

Temporary manpower services can offer a large number of laborers on very short notices, at modest fees. In many cases a good temporary worker will become a good full-time employee.

Using a Blind Box

Use of a "blind box" in the classified section of the newspaper is one way to obtain resumes for various positions without publicizing the name of your company. It is particularly advantageous to use "blind box" advertisements when it is suspected that an employee in a crucial position may be leaving. The advertisement can be coded to identify the publication it appeared in, or the date of the publication. For example "Box 6O6T5Pr" could signify that envelopes received are responding to an ad placed in the *Times* on the fifth day of the month, for the production department.

At least twice per year an attempt should be made to evaluate the relative merits of the various sources of personnel through objective measurement. A table can be developed which compares turnover, grievances and disciplinary action for example, with the hiring sources. Such comparisons and tabulations, while not conclusive because of many other factors, can give valuable information in areas that may otherwise be difficult to assess objectively.

Now let's examine interviewing and reference checking in Chapters Three and Four.

CHART 3
APPLICATION FOR EMPLOYMENT

NAME: _____

ADDRESS: _____

HOME TELEPHONE: _____ BUSINESS TELEPHONE: _____

SOCIAL SECURITY NUMBER: _____

DATE OF BIRTH (OPTIONAL): _____ U.S. CITIZEN: ☐ YES ☐ NO

Position(s) applied for _____

Rate of pay expected $ _____ per week

Applying for Full-Time _____ Part-Time _____ Specify days and hours if

part-time _____

Were you previously employed by us? _____ If yes, when? _____

How did you hear of us? _____

Date available for work? _____ 19_____

EDUCATION

COLLEGE ATTENDED	ADDRESS	YEARS ATTENDED	DEGREE AND YEAR
_____	_____	_____	_____
_____	_____	_____	_____
_____	_____	_____	_____

HIGH SCHOOL	ADDRESS	YEAR GRADUATED
_____	_____	_____

OTHER	ADDRESS	SUBJECT STUDIED
_____	_____	_____

24

PREVIOUS EMPLOYMENT

JOB TITLE:_____ SALARY:_____

NAME OF COMPANY:_____

ADDRESS:_____

NAME OF IMMEDIATE SUPERVISOR:_____ TEL:_____

MAY WE CONTACT: ☐ YES ☐ NO

DESCRIPTION OF DUTIES:_____

_____

_____

REASON FOR LEAVING:_____

EMPLOYED FROM _____ TO _____

JOB TITLE:_____ SALARY:_____

NAME OF COMPANY:_____

ADDRESS:_____

NAME OF IMMEDIATE SUPERVISOR:_____ TEL:_____

MAY WE CONTACT: ☐ YES ☐ NO

DESCRIPTION OF DUTIES:_____

_____

_____

REASON FOR LEAVING:_____

EMPLOYED FROM _____ TO _____

JOB TITLE:_____ SALARY:_____

NAME OF COMPANY:_____

ADDRESS:_____

NAME OF IMMEDIATE SUPERVISOR:_____ TEL:_____

MAY WE CONTACT: ☐ YES ☐ NO

DESCRIPTION OF DUTIES:_____

_____

_____

REASON FOR LEAVING:_____

EMPLOYED FROM_____ TO_____

Please use additional paper if necessary.

Please list other experiences, skills, or qualifications_____

_____

_____

_____

The information set forth in this employment application is accurate
and complete. I hereby authorize any investigation of my educational and
professional history through investigative agencies or bureaus. I
acknowledge that if employed, any false or misleading information presented on this employment application is sufficient cause for dismissal.

_____ _____
Signature   Date

26

CHART 4

INTERVIEW RATING

POSITION APPLIED FOR	NAME
DEPARTMENT	ADDRESS
	TOWN ZIP
	PHONE

AREA	RATING
INTERPERSONAL SKILLS	1 2 3 4 5 6 7 8 9 10
ARTICULATION	1 2 3 4 5 6 7 8 9 10
APPEARANCE	1 2 3 4 5 6 7 8 9 10
POISE	1 2 3 4 5 6 7 8 9 10
AMBITION	1 2 3 4 5 6 7 8 9 10
EXPERIENCE	1 2 3 4 5 6 7 8 9 10
EDUCATION	1 2 3 4 5 6 7 8 9 10
SPECIAL TRAINING	1 2 3 4 5 6 7 8 9 10
OVERALL QUALIFICATIONS	1 2 3 4 5 6 7 8 9 10

Comments _____

_____

_____

_____

_____

DATE	REVIEWER

CHAPTER THREE

INTERVIEWING MADE EASY

Jane Milner had recently been appointed as director of administration for a New York City advertising and public relations agency. In her new position, Jane was responsible for interviewing job candidates. She was fairly confident that she could effectively conduct a 30–45 minute interview with any prospect who came through her door, and thus didn't feel the need to prepare questions in advance, or to undertake any preparation for that matter.

Five weeks to the day after she was hired, Jane had responsibility for interviewing candidates for an new position that had opened up with the agency. It took Jane only 45 minutes—the length of the first interview she conducted—to realize that preparation was indeed necessary. The interview was a shambles, Jane was nervous, lost track of what she was telling the prospect, and poorly represented the agency.

In this chapter we'll examine practical methods for preparing and conducting interviews. We'll also focus on the following questions:

☐ What should be done **before the applicant arrives**?
☐ What is a **question funnel**?
☐ **When** should the applicant be **rated**?
☐ What are some **questions** that can be asked of the applicant during the interview?
☐ What **steps** should you take **following the interview**?

Get Ready, Get Set

Before the applicant arrives, plans should be made to structure the interview. It should be decided in advance what the objectives are, such as whether someone is wanted with long-range potential or growth potential. The job description will provide guidelines as to what the objectives of the interview should be. It is also important for the supervisor to know the position **thoroughly** and be able to describe the qualities that are essential for successful performance.

Attempt to create a "**question funnel**" which involves beginning with broad relevant questions, working toward the specific. To build trust, always pose a positive question before a negative one. The phrasing of questions should not be threatening. If one must probe for details, stick to "echoing," which is making a question out of the applicant's last statement, or use the neutral "tell me more" question.

A strong attempt should be made to be **consistent with each candidate**, in order that comparison with other candidates will be valid. Notes should be taken during the interview period, but not during tense moments. For a good interview, the questions should be well-planned and there should be a true interest in what the applicant says.

Immediately following the interview, rate the applicant objectively. The rating can be as simple as below average, average, above average for abilities, training or traits that are essential for the position. Many interviewers use a 1 to 5, or a 1 to 10 scale to rate applicants. The method used for rating can vary; what is important is that **criteria essential for the** position is used and that the method for **rating is as objective as possible**.

The following interview questions are presented for a handy guide:

Accomplishment and Goals
- ☐ How do you deal with people most effectively?
- ☐ What new skills or experience would you like to acquire in the immediate future?
- ☐ Cite your latest major career achievement?
- ☐ What problems have you solved that were plaguing your organization?
- ☐ What do you do best?
- ☐ What do you prefer to do?
- ☐ Why are you seeking to change jobs? Or, what type of job are you applying for?
- ☐ Do you prefer long-term assignments or short assignments with quick feedback?
- ☐ How do you feel you could best contribute here?
- ☐ What leadership have you assumed in the past?

Education
- [ ] Why did you choose the school that you went to?
- [ ] What were your favorite/least favorite courses?
- [ ] What level of effort was needed to achieve those grades?
- [ ] What special projects or independent studies did you undertake?
- [ ] What courses you would like to take in the future?
- [ ] How did you pay for your education?
- [ ] Looking back, would you choose the same school and courses?
- [ ] What was your grade point average?

General
- [ ] Do you have any involvement in community organizations?
- [ ] What are your hobbies/interests?
- [ ] What would others say about your work or work habits?
- [ ] How well do you take constructive criticism?
- [ ] Do you get frustrated occasionally or do you tend to usually stay calm?
- [ ] What do you know about our company?
- [ ] In a sentence, why are you the best candidate for the position?

What If Your Undecided about a Candidate?

Now, here's another job interview checklist of tough questions from William A. Cohen, author of *The Executive's Guide to Finding a Superior Job*.

This checklist is useful if you're undecided about a particular applicant or if the job to be filled requires a very special person.

CHART 5
TOUGH QUESTIONS TO ASK A JOB CANDIDATE
- [ ] What's wrong with your present job?
- [ ] Does your boss know you are looking for a job?
- [ ] Why have you made so many job changes?
- [ ] Why are you interested in our company?
- [ ] How ambitious are you?
- [ ] What are your three greatest strengths, in order?
- [ ] What are your three greatest weaknesses, in order?
- [ ] Where do you want to be in five years?
- [ ] Where do you think you'll be?
- [ ] Are you technically or management oriented?
- [ ] Do you feel you have top management potential? Why?

- [ ] How good a worker are you? Details?
- [ ] How good a leader are you ? Details?
- [ ] What have you disliked most about past jobs?
- [ ] What do you think you would like best about this job?
- [ ] How important to you is salary compared to other aspects of the job?
- [ ] What does the word success mean to you?
- [ ] What types of jobs are you looking for?
- [ ] Why aren't you making more money?
- [ ] Why should we be interested in hiring you?

If you or your organization are unsure as to what may and may not be asked during a job interview, *Employees' Rights in Plain English* by Joel D. Joseph, National Press, is a useful and effective guide.

Who's Looking for a Job

It is helpful to know why the applicants are seeking a position with your organization. Some applicants may have left their former job because they could not get along with the boss. They will not mention this immediately, because they feel it will make them look bad. Rather than criticize their former boss, they will cite differences of policy or principle. If additional questioning reveals that they simply did not get along with their boss, do not downgrade the applicant for not admitting that up front; few will. This individual may do a good job.

Often one encounters applicants that have been in many organizations—none of them for long. This may indicate personality problems, lack of direction, or simply an avoidance of responsibility and hard work on a sustained basis. It is best to stay away from applicants who have had several positions of short duration. Also avoid applicants who stress "who they know" rather than what they have accomplished or are able to accomplish.

An applicant who has done his/her homework; someone who knows about the company or your department, as strategist Pete R. Johnson advocates or has taken the time to assess what your needs may be, should be given extra consideration. Many applicants, in essence, are asking, "What do you have for me?" Thus, it is refreshing to encounter an applicant who says "This is how I can contribute," or "Here is where I think I can benefit the organization."

CHART 6

Inquiries Before Hiring	Lawful	Unlawful to ask if used for discrimination
• Name	Name	Inquiry into any title that indicates race, color, religion, sex, national origin, or ancestry
• Address	Inquiry into place and length of time at previous addresses	Specific inquiry into foreign or current addresses that would indicate national origin
• Age	A. Request proof of age in form of work permit issued by school authorities B. Require proof of age by birth certificate after hiring	Require birth certificate or baptismal record before hiring
• Birthplace or national origin		A. Any inquiry into place of birth B. Any inquiry into place of parents, grandparents, or spouse C. Any other inquiry into national origin
• Race or color		Any inquiry which would indicate race or color
• Religion/creed		A. Any inquiry to indicate or identify denomination or customs B. May not be told this is a protestant (Catholic or Jewish) organization C. Request pastor's recommendation or reference
• Citizenship	A. Whether a U.S. citizen B. If not, whether intends become one C. If U.S. residence is legal D. If spouse is citizen E. Require proof of citizenship after hiring	A. If native born or naturalized B. Proof of citizenship before hiring C. Whether parents or spouse are native born or naturalized

32

Inquiries Before Hiring	Lawful	Unlawful to ask if used for discrimination
• Photographs	May be required after hiring for identification purposes	Request photograph before hiring
• Education	A. Inquiry into what academic, professional or vocational schools attended B. Inquiry into language skills such as ability to read and write foreign languages	A. Any inquiry asking specifically the racial or religious affiliation of a school B. Inquiry as to what is mother tongue or how foreign language ability was acquired, unless necessary for job
• Relatives	Inquiry into name, relationship and address of person to be notified in case of emergency	Any inquiry about a relative that is un-lawful to ask about the applicant
• Organization	A. Inquiry into organization memberships, excluding any organization the name or character of which indicates the race, color, religion, sex, national origin or ancestry of its members. B. What offices are held, if any	Inquiry into *all* and organizations where membership is held
• Military service	A. Inquiry into service in U.S. Armed Services B. Rank attained C. Which branch of service D. Require military discharge certificate after being hired	A. Inquiry into military service in armed service if any country but U.S. B. Request military service records
• Work Schedule	Inquiry into willingness to work required schedule	Any inquiry into willingness to work any particular religious holiday
• Other qualifications	Any questions that have direct reflection on the job applied for	Any non-job related inquiry that may suggest unlawful discrimination
• References	General personal and work references not relating to race, color, sex national origin or ancestry	Request references specifically from clergy or any other persons who might reflect race, color, religion, sex, national origin or ancestry of applicant

Reasons for Not Hiring

Discussion with supervisors, personnel managers and others with hiring responsibilities reveals many common factors regarding why applicants are not hired. Often the key reason for not hiring stems from one of the following:

- ☐ The personal **"chemistry"** between applicant and interviewer **was not right.**
- ☐ The applicant **has had too many jobs** without accompanying upward movement.
- ☐ An **agreement on salary** could not be reached.
- ☐ A reference check revealed that the applicant had a **poor employment record.**
- ☐ The applicant **interviewed poorly.**

Other reasons that were cited less often include the applicant not having "the right background" or not seeming to have "sufficient growth potential."

But beware, the criteria you use to hire new employees may be irrelevant and could actually produce an inferior workforce. Drs. Herbert and Jeanne Greenberg of Personality Dynamics, Inc., Princeton, NJ interviewed more than 360,000 employees and applicants over a 19 year period and found that "external qualities so long used as 'knock-out' or selection factors do not hold up" as reliable employment evaluators.

The Greenbergs believe that experience has as little to do with eventual success on the job as do sex, age, race, formal education and the other items mentioned above. "How often is ten years experience simply one year's **bad** experience repeated ten times?" They say their study turned up an abundance of repeated bad experiences ... apparently, failures by supervisors and their employees to correct past mistakes.

"What counts are the **dynamics within** a human being that make him or her appropriate or not appropriate for a particular job," according to the researchers. "If industry will match an individual's personality to the real requirements of the job ... increased productivity, reduced turnover, and better job satisfaction can be assured."

Interview Follow-Up

As a follow-up to the initial interview the following recommendations are made for applicants for which there is strong interest:

☐ Make a reference check (see page 36)
☐ When possible, arrange a second interview and have other employees interview applicants.

No one should be hired on the spot; wait a while so that the applicant has adequate time to consider the situation and so that an increased measure of objectivity can be gained during that time.

After interviewing a strong candidate for an open position, it is a good idea to have the job candidate formulate his/her own job description based on what he/she has learned about the job. At a second interview, review the candidate's job description and compare it with your original description. If the differences in the job description interpretations are mutually resolved (given that all other factors have been considered), a hire/no-hire decision can be made.

In the next chapter we'll examine the oh, so important responsibility of checking references.

CHAPTER FOUR

CHECKING REFERENCES

The need to check references of job applicants is becoming increasingly apparent. As will be discussed in Chapter Six, "Spotting Phony Resumes," more than a few of the job applicants that you'll encounter will misrepresent themselves in some way on their resume or application form.

Independent of any misrepresentation, it makes excellent sense to get in touch with the references offered by job applicants because a substantial body of useful information on the applicant can be gleaned quickly. This chapter will provide information on how to effectively check references and verify other information submitted by applicants. We'll also provide answers to the following questions:

☐ Why is it better to phone rather than write to references?
☐ How can you quickly gain the information you need to help assess the suitability of job applicants?
☐ What type of conversational tone is best to obtain useful information from a previous employer?
☐ What does a long-winded, uninformative answer to one of your questions often mean?
☐ Why should other references be sought, beyond those listed by the applicant?

Get'em On The Phone

You've interviewed someone who seems just right for the job. But, you recognize that it's still important and revealing to make a reference check. If at all possible, make telephone reference checks rather than seeking information by mail. Why? Because more information can be obtained in a shorter time period by phone. Few people are willing to put negative comments on paper. Also, voice cues are extremely helpful.

When calling references speak slowly and assuredly offering your name, position and company and the reason why you're calling, i.e., "John Smith has given us your name as a reference."

If you have a checklist to work from, your time and effectiveness on the telephone will be greatly enhanced. (See chart 7)

What to Ask

Listed below are 15 points which will enable you to gain a wealth of information on job applicants.

1. Employment dates? What are the exact dates of the applicant's employment with your organization/company/department/firm?
2. Initial job? What were the applicant's initial responsibilities when starting work with you?
3. Ending job? What were the applicant's current or last responsibilities on the job?
4. Supervisory need? What level of supervision did the applicant require?
5. Team member? Did the applicant prefer to work as part of a team or on his/her own?
6. Conflicts encountered? What work/job/career related conflicts did the applicant encounter?
7. Attendance/absenteeism?—What was the applicant's record of attendance?
8. Strengths?—Can you cite three to five of the applicant's strengths?
9. Weaknesses?—Can you cite three to five of the applicant's weaknesses?
10. Learning capability?—Does the applicant possess quick learning ability? If not, adequate learning ability?
11. Record compared to others?—What is the applicant's record compared to others, i.e., peers, co-workers, those with similar duties or responsibilities?
12. Why leaving?—Based on your knowledge, why did the applicant depart (or why is the applicant departing) your organization?
13. How replaced?—How will you replace the applicant upon his/her departure?
14. Parting compensation?—What is the final compensation earned by the applicant in your organization?

15. Would you rehire?—Given your experience with the applicant and in recognition of job requirements, would you
rehire the applicant?

In addition, here are other questions you may wish to pose to
references which will shed even further light on a job applicant's
capabilities and suitability for the position available with you.
- ☐ Could you please rank the applicant's responsibilities in
descending order?
- ☐ What is the best way to work with the applicant for his/her
greatest effectiveness and output?
- ☐ What could the applicant have done to have been more
successful?
- ☐ How would you describe the applicant's overall attitude?
- ☐ What additional training, courses, or activity does the applicant need for continued development?

Listen Between the Lines

An increase in litigation has made former employers cautious
of saying anything negative about former employees. Thus it is of
great importance to "listen between the lines;" rely on your own
instincts of what the reference is really telling you. For example,
less than glowing praise regarding an applicant's record compared to others may well mean the applicant is mediocre. The
same holds true for a long winded response that really doesn't
answer your question. Less than an immediate "yes," to the question: "Would you rehire this person?" can well mean "no."

CHART 7

TELEPHONE REFERENCE CHECKLIST

APPLICANT NAME_____ REFERENCE NAME_____

STREET_____ TITLE_____

TOWN, CITY, ZIP_____ COMPANY_____

PHONE NUMBER_____ STREET_____

DATE_____ TOWN, STATE, ZIP_____

PHONE NUMBER_____

1. Employment dates?_____

_____

2. Initial responsibilities?_____

_____

3. Ending responsibilities?_____

_____

4. Supervisory needs?_____

_____

5. Team member?_____

_____

6. Conflicts encountered?_____

_____

7. Attendance/absenteeism?_____

_____

8. Strengths (3-5)?_____

_____

9. Weaknesses (3-5)?_____

_____

10. Learning capability?_____

_____

11. Record compared to others?_____

_____

12. Why leaving?_____

_____

13. How replaced?_____

_____

14. Parting compensation?_____

_____

15. Would you re-hire?_____

_____

If You Can't Call, Write

It's likely that you can't get nearly the same amount of information by writing as by calling for several reasons: 1. No one likes to take the time to write the responses to your questions; 2. As previously stated, no one likes to put negative reports in writing; and 3. Writing provides no voice cues.

If you have trouble contacting a reference by phone, the chart below, "Mail Reference Check" can be used. Note particularly the comment section as some may be offered in the case of outstanding employees.

Remember that many references have built-in biases. Some people have very little good to say about anyone. Some employers feel scorned that the employee left them. Still others always generalize when asked specifically about someone else's performance.

To get the most mileage out of a reference check, particularly if it's the applicant's previous employer, it's essential to establish a cordial, vibrant conversation.

CHART 8

MAIL REFERENCE CHECK

_____   _____

DATE

_____

RE: EVALUATION OF

_____

_____   _____

Dear_____

We are presently in the process of evaluating many candidates for the position of _____ in our _____ office.

40

In order that we make an intelligent selection that also benefits the individual chosen, could you please take a few minutes to objectively assess _____ based on your first-hand experience in working with him/her. For your convenience you may return this letter. Thank you for your cooperation.

Yours truly,

	(lowest)							(highest)	
	1	2	3	4	5	6	7	8	9	10
energy, enthusiasm										
output, productivity										
dependability										
ability to handle pressure										
attendance										
learning capability										
overall value to org.										

COMMENTS _____

_____

_____

The Extra Effort

In addition to checking the references submitted by the applicant, make the extra effort to get in touch with the applicant's former bosses or supervisors, co-workers, and others that may not have been listed as references but who can offer very revealing information.

A Reoccurring Theme

It's a reoccurring theme throughout this book that management/supervision and employee communications is a dynamic process and the ebb and flow of employees in the workplace continues unabated. Thus, checking references is now a mandatory function of the candidate   selection process as it clearly increases the probability of hiring capable, responsible employees.

When possible, arrange a second interview with the applicant particularly after references have been checked to get a more rounded, objective view of the applicant.

No one should ever be hired on the spot, even if it's a second interview and all the references have checked out marvelously. As a professional courtesy, one to two weeks consideration time should always be offered.

Here's a checklist of key points made in the chapter:

- ☐ Make telephone reference checks rather than seeking information by mail.
- ☐ Work from a prepared telephone reference checklist.
- ☐ Listen between the lines of what the reference is telling you.
- ☐ Use a mail reference check when you have trouble contacting a reference by phone.
- ☐ Make an extra effort to get in touch with the applicant's former bosses, supervisors, etc.
- ☐ Do not hire anyone on the spot. Offer one to two weeks consideration time.

In Chapter Five, "Acknowledging Built-in Turnover Factors," we'll examine why some apparent good hires end up leaving in short order!

CHAPTER FIVE

ACKNOWLEDGING BUILT-IN TURNOVER FACTORS

Walter Ross had always prided himself on his ability to assist in the selection of the right type of worker for his department. When a recent job opening developed, Walter carefully reassessed the skills and abilities necessary to successfully handle the position. Walter was instrumental in the selection of Al Morris, who would be handling some key accounts.

In the weeks that followed Al made reasonable progress, yet did not seem particularly happy in his new position. One morning Al approached Walter and told him that "things just weren't working out." He then promptly resigned. Walter was stunned. Yet with a little more research into Al's recent job experience the situation might have been avoided.

In this chapter we'll answer the questions:

☐ Why do so many **new hires turnover** in short order?

☐ What are **five** potential **built-in turnover factors** that can be spotted early?

☐ What type of employee generally requires a more **structured organization**?

☐ How will knowing potential built-in causes of turnover help to **reduce** overall turnover?

A Mass Exodus

Why do so many hires with seemingly adequate or even superior capabilities turnover in less than a year, (and too often in a matter of months)? Frequently the reason is that one of several factors existed at the outset that all but guaranteed a rapid departure.

Even if all goes well in hiring and it appears that a good position to job candidate match has been made, there may be trouble in the coming months if any one of the following circumstances is present:

- [ ] someone is hired for **less compensation** than he/she previously achieved
- [ ] a new hire **does not have supervisory responsibilities** but previously did
- [ ] the position does not represent **forward movement** for the new employee
- [ ] the new hire requires a **highly structured, organizational setting**, or
- [ ] a **clear, mutual understanding** of job responsibilities was never established.

Let's examine these five factors that H. Edward Muendel, an Annapolis based executive search consultant, has termed "built-in turnover factors."

Hired for Less Compensation

Remember the scene in *Kramer vs. Kramer* when Dustin Hoffman sits patiently at an office Christmas party, waiting to hear if he's going to instantly land a job for $4800 *less* than he made at his last job?

An employee hired for less compensation or the same compensation that he/she made previously often spells trouble. No one likes to work for less than they made before and, given the creeping, if not relentless increase in the cost of living, earning the same amount that you made before is also working for less.

An employee who does take a job under this compensation structure, shortly is not going to be happy as he/she sees his purchasing power decline. Moreover, an employee who does take compensation under this arrangement may be merely taking a position for the quick cash that can be generated, while continuing to seek a position for greater compensation. Generally, it is not recommended to hire someone who is willing to accept a salary that is less than or equal to what they have made previously.

.... OF COURSE YOU'LL BE MAKING CONSIDERABLY LESS THAN YOUR LAST JOB, BUT THE WORK, OF COURSE, WILL BE MUCH MORE CHALLENGING ...

No Supervisory Responsibilities

A new employee who does not have supervisory responsibilities, but formerly had them, may soon feel frustrated. If an employee is hired who previously managed a department of ten to twelve people, for example, and is now joining your company as a staff person with authority over no one else, it won't be long before this individual misses the responsibility and control that had been attained on the previous job. (Unless, of course, in a previous position he/she had an extreme disliking for managing others or is semi-retired and not interested in maintaining heavy responsibilities.)

No Forward Movement

If the position does not represent a move upward or a new career for the new employee—again, problems may soon develop. If the employee accepts a position with your business that represents a lateral movement, you may later find that you have hired someone who intends to "coast"or "retire"on the job; we have come to expect that most career minded individuals seek at least a slightly better job than the one that they previously had.

Structured Position Required

Some employees require a highly structured position in an organizational network. For example, it is difficult for some individuals to move from a large corporation to a small firm. In a large corporation there were systems and procedures to be followed for every facet of operations. In the smaller firm, SBA management developed specialist Joseph V. Casamento says, much of the red tape, corporate procedure and paper shuffling may be diminished.

Many employees who previously worked in larger corporate settings found comfort in the systems and paper work and, surprisingly, will not function as effectively in a more loosely structured business environment. In addition, the larger organization had a fully established network and hierarchy of positions through which the employee could fully understand how he/she fit into the organizational network. In a smaller organization this may not be clear and may be unsettling to some employees.

Mutual Understanding Not Established

Psychologist and trainer Paul O. Radde, Ph.D., asks, "How often is a clear, mutual understanding of a job's tasks and responsibilities established by a supervisor and new employee?" Thousands of times each day across the nation a new hire leaves a company because a job turned out to be something that was entirely different from what he/she originally had conceived. This has to be the responsibility of the interviewers and managers/supervisors who initiated the hiring in the first place.

Conclusion

There are literally hundreds of reasons why new employees don't work out. The five discussed in this chapter at a minimum, provide a base or frame of reference from which you, as supervisor, can begin to alleviate the turnover problem.

In the next chapter we'll focus on the increasing incidence of phony resumes and how to avoid hiring someone who uses one!

Later, in Section VI, we'll examine how to handle the departure of good employees.

CHAPTER SIX

SPOTTING PHONY RESUMES

Phony resumes, or at least those that contain misrepresentations, are nothing new to the working world, but in times of economic fluctuation appear with increasing frequency. According to Camden and Associates, a leading employment agency, nearly eighty percent of all resumes contain at least some misleading information, usually in the area of employment history. "The most common misrepresentation occurs when candidates fabricate names of firms they worked for to cover long gaps of unemployment."

This chapter will focus on these key areas:

☐ Why do more and more applicants make phony claims or misrepresentations on their resumes?

☐ Why are no gaps in an individual's employment record a possible clue to misrepresentation?

☐ How can school attendance and courses be inflated on the resume?

☐ Why should you be weary of achievements stated in non-specific terminology?

☐ How can you quickly verify resume information during the interview?

A Frequent Phenomenon

Selecting the right job applicant for a position can be a costly and time-consuming process. As the number of resumes or job applicants increases dramatically compared to the number of advertised job openings, applicants are naturally eager to present themselves via a cover letter and resume in the best possible way. Knowing that competition is keen, many resort to "improving" their resumes through misrepresentation, fabrication and outright fraud.

Supervisors, personnel officers and top management from large organizations to the very smallest are generally cognizant of the phony resume phenomenon. However, few interviewers have the time to verify fully an applicant's resume and when verification is done, it consumes time and money. Let's examine some ways to spot a phony resume or, at least, to alert oneself to the possibility thereof, thus conserving resources and enhancing movement toward the selection of the truly best job applicant.

No Employment Gaps

For entry level type job applicants as well as more senior individuals with at least five to seven years of employment experience, the odds are that there has been some unemployment or down time. A resume which indicates an air-tight chronological sequence of employment with no gaps is actually the exception rather than the rule these days. One familiar technique used by many resume preparers is to offer job histories by years as opposed to by month and year. This, of course, affords one the opportunity to disguise as much as twelve months or more of unemployment or other activity. Similarly, individuals who have been self-employed, worked in a family-owned business or had a previous employer who subsequently went out of business are afforded somewhat of an opportunity to arrange creatively the dates of their employment history.

..NEUROSURGERY AT ST. SIDNEY'S, BUSBOY AT HARDEES, CHAIRMAN OF THE BOARD FOR EXXON .... FIRST SECRETARY OF THE COMMUNIST PARTY OF THE SOVIET UNION & CARPENTER'S HELPER ...

Citing Colleges But Not the Type of Degree

Now and then a resume may cross your desk in which a job applicant has cited the name of the university he/she attended without accompanying information as to the type of degree or major subject area. If one is to meet this individual the remedy is, of course, to ask for this additional information and, even better, to ask for a transcript copy.

I've also found it curious over the years that so many individuals in the world graduated from Harvard or Stanford—or the like. I finally concluded that when phonies set out to prepare a resume, they go for the best, or at least what they perceive to be the best, or what they perceive will get them the furthest. Again, a request for a transcript settles all.

Inflating Specialized Courses

Related to the issue of not fully identifying one's educational background is the rather common practice of inflating specialized courses taken to make it appear as if one attended a particular university for full four years or for a full graduate program. The MBA or graduate business school program of several top universities now offer executive development programs or project management and marketing programs which require six to eight weeks of intensive on-sight study. Generally, these are excellent programs. Often, however, graduations from these limited programs are conveyed on some individuals' resumes as if the course work involved much more or yielded a graduate or undergraduate degree rather than just a certificate.

I knew of one individual who now heads his own management consulting firm in Chicago who received a Bachelor of Science in Business Administration and an MBA from a small college in the midwest. He then attended an executive development program from a major northeastern university and thereafter presented his educational background in a manner that would lead most people to believe he received his MBA from the major northeastern university. When confronted with these facts he is quick to avoid explanation—and continues to use the same deceptive wording in his corporate brochure.

Many resume preparers who have attended but one summer, adult, weekend, or extension course of a major university present such on the resume as "attended University of ————." This too is outright misrepresentation.

Citing Achievements With Broad-Based Numerical Ranges

Have you ever examined the resume that included phrases such as the following:

— "saved the company over one million dollars . . ."
— "did 100% over quota . . ."
— "increased market share by more than 15%. . . ."

Anyone of the above constitutes a lofty achievement, and there is no reason that the individual citing such an achievement could not give more specific figures. As a rule of thumb, terminology such as more than, over than, greater than, rather than the precise figure is a signal that exaggeration and misrepresentation may be occurring.

A Problem Here to Stay

It's not likely that the incidence of phony resume preparation is going to decrease in the near future. Moreover, even if you're a pro at spotting what appears to be a misrepresentative resume, undoubtedly more than a few will slip by you without being detected. While it's far more costly and time-consuming to conduct an interview with a job applicant than to simply review or read his/her resume, in terms of verifying resume information it's far easier during an interview.

To verify educational background data with fairly recent college graduates, you might try the following: "I see you went to X University. Were you there when Dean Adams headed your school? " The truthful applicant will state the name of the dean who served while he/she attended that university. The phony will hem and haw, state that he/she can't remember or provide some other vague response such as "I think so," " I'm not sure" or "I'll have to check." If you doubt that asking for the name of one's dean in college is not a fair test, pose the question to your junior staff members or co-workers and you'll quickly see that most or all are readily able to recall the name.

The Award Winning Candidate

Another ploy of phonies is to create a list of awards and honors that they've received or to cite various publications. The easiest way to confirm this information is to request documentation or copies of such items while on the phone with the applicant to arrange the interview. Here again, an applicant that has truly won such and such awards or had articles published in various journals will be able to supply documentation and will do so gladly. The phony may become uneasy when such requests are made during the initial phone call and will undoubtedly have an excuse during the interview as to why the materials could not be produced.

I have never met an individual who having written a published article and listed it on his/her resume was not able to readily supply me with at least a photocopy.

While it's not always possible to spot a phony resume, steps can be taken to ensure that the number of phony resumes received is reduced. Many organizations have stated their policy regarding fraud or misrepresentation on job application forms. One could even make reference to this policy in newspaper employment advertisements. Finally, the policy could be simply stated in a clause or paragraph which accompanies all correspondence with new job applicants.

If some of the items discussed above seem like added burdens, then consider the added burden to you and your organization when you hire the wrong person for the job based partially on the phony resume that he/she submitted.

Here's a checklist for quickly checking up on that "too good to be true" resume:

- ☐ Are there gaps in employment? This is very probable these days.
- ☐ Are schools and universities cited with no mention of degree earned? Maybe he/she never got one.
- ☐ Does the candidate seem to have a phenomenal educational background? It could be a case of inflated specialized courses.
- ☐ Are achievements cited with glossover terminology, such as "saved more than"?
- ☐ Can the applicant name specific people from his/her past such as the dean of the college, or editor of the journal in which he/she was published?
- ☐ Can the applicant provide documentation regarding awards received or articles published?

In the next chapter we'll examine applicants' resumes even more closely—not for misrepresentation—but for telltale signs that may signal disqualification.

OH YEAH... SURE... I DOUBLED.. NO... QUADRUPLED MY COMPANIES SALES IN JUST TWO SHORT WEEKS..... MAYBE I TRIPLED... I FORGET....

PERSONNEL

CHAPTER SEVEN

READING BETWEEN THE LINES OF RESUMES

Resumes are designed to contain useful information concerning the qualifications of job applicants. By carefully examining resumes further, however, one can gain valuable clues indicating which applicants should be disqualified beyond those that have used outright misrepresentation. The job of selecting the most qualified applicant for a position is never easy. Being able to readily remove marginal applicants from consideration will, at the very least, enhance the selection process.

This chapter discusses six techniques for "reading between the lines" of a resume and answers these questions:

- [ ] What can the **quality of copy** used for a resume tell you about the applicant?
- [ ] Is a **long list of outside hobbies** and interests helpful or harmful for future performance?
- [ ] Does use of **non-traditional sized or colored paper** yield important information?
- [ ] What **type of stationery** used should automatically disqualify a job applicant?
- [ ] Why, unfortunately, is it often necessary to eliminate many applicants quickly via **clues from the resume**?

A Copy of a Copy

There's nothing wrong in particular about a resume that has been photocopied. With the wide installation of high speed quality copiers more and more people are using photocopiers rather than going to an off-set printer. A warning buzzer should go off, however, when you examine a resume that appears to be a second or third generation photocopy, or a "copy of a copy." If a job applicant and potential employee will submit a resume that has a poor appearance or is shoddy, it is likely that when hired he/she will take short-cuts on the job.

Many-believe that disqualifying an applicant for sending a copy of a copy is too stern a measure. However, the image that one conveys, especially via written correspondence, is important and undoubtedly will provide clues as to future behavior.

Over-listing of Outside Activities

There's nothing necessarily wrong with someone who belongs to a wide variety of civic, professional, recreational and social groups. An over-listing of these types of activities, however, may indicate that the person is a "joiner" and not a "doer." Someone who is over-engaged in outside activities may be providing an indication that, once hired, will provide only a minimum of effort on the job.

One other potential problem with an individual who has over-listed activities is that he/she may lack the ability to focus attention on specific areas of interest. This section of the resume must be examined closely since there is a fine line between an active, industrious person and an overbooked socialite.

Ambiguous Dates in Employment History

It's no longer a business or professional stigma to have a gap in employment dates. Gaps represent the rule rather than the exception. A problem exists when a resume contains ambiguous information regarding the dates of the applicant's employment. Be wary of a resume that contains only yearly information and not month and year, or if the timing of the transition from one job to the next is so smooth so as to possibly be contrived.

An Overly-long Resume

An overly-long resume, especially one that contains a long list of achievements, could spell trouble. On paper, it's easy enough to beef up anything anyone has ever done. When reviewing awards or achievements cited, focus more on quality—what was accomplished, for whom and in what time period—rather than quantity of items listed. Also, keep in mind that the industry and company from which an applicant came, may have been in the practice of making periodic awards. Thus, an individual's ability to list awards and achievements may be more contingent upon where he/she worked rather than what he/she accomplished.

Unusual Sizes or Colors of Papers

Most serious applicants will conform to the norm of 8 & 1/2 x 11 paper that is white or off-white in color. Acceptable alternatives to white include light beige, light gold, and, possibly very light green or very light blue. A resume presented on loud or garishly colored paper is a strong indication that the applicant is not serious about employment with your company or the applicant simply has poor taste. Exceptions include creative-type positions within advertising or the communications industry or positions in the entertainment field.

The size of the paper used is also important. Occasionally one observes a resume on 9″ x 12″ paper or on 8 1/2 x 14″ paper legal size. There's nothing particularly wrong with use of odd size paper, but again, most serious applicants would not take the chance of exhibiting non-conformity in the application process. One may assume that the most qualified applicants are likely to submit resumes on 8 & 1/2″ x 11″ paper.

Use of Company Stationery

I once received a resume in the mail from a young lady working for Pittsburgh Plate Glass (PPG). But what was really surprising is that she used a PPG envelope! Needless to say, she was immediately placed among the disqualified.

A resume, cover letter or envelope that bears the logo, trademark, or insignia of an applicant's current or, perhaps, former company is a dead give-away that this applicant should be disqualified. Use of anyone's stationery but one's own in submitting a resume is totally inappropriate and offers a keen indication of the future practices of this person were he/she to be hired by you.

Here's a quick checklist for reading between the lines of resumes.

☐ Beware of copies of copies
☐ Reassess the potential of the over-joiner
☐ Be wary of ambiguous dates in employment history
☐ Question the need for an overly long resume
☐ Discount resumes on loud or garishly colored paper
☐ Disqualify resumes using the stationery of former employers

The task of selecting the best person for a position is often difficult, especially in today's job market when any solicitation for resumes is likely to incur an avalanche of them. Unfortunately, the fastest way to narrow down the pile is to eliminate those resumes which, for whatever reason, yield information that disqualify the applicant. It is possible that the resume of a perfectly qualified applicant could contain some of the problems cited above. For purposes of efficiency, however, and reliance upon probability, "reading between the lines" of resumes will help you to get to the final selection faster.

CHAPTER EIGHT

BRINGING A NEW EMPLOYEE ON BOARD

Once hired and ready to begin work, a new employee's first impression is very important and can often have a strong and lasting effect on the employee's morale. Supplying new employees with all the information they need to feel that they "belong" is essential. It has been demonstrated that the dividends in good will, morale, and production efficiency greatly outweigh the effort required to make a new employee feel at home.

Many companies have developed a comprehensive orientation procedure. For smaller companies, it is not necessary to establish elaborate procedures; the use of a simple orientation checklist will suffice.

In this chapter we'll review the steps for effectively orienting a new employee to your staff and the organization. Also, here are some questions that will be answered:

□ What should new employee orientation consist of, at a minimum?
□ Why is it important to structure the time of the new hire?
□ What do orientation checklists contain ?
□ What is a probationary period and why is it useful?

Minimum Requirements

Orientation should, at the minimum, include the following:

□ Introduction to other employees;
□ Tour of facilities;
□ Check-in procedures:
  — Use of time cards (if applicable);
  — Issuance of keys, supplies, etc.;

59

- Compensation policy: when paid, deductions taken;
- Call-in procedures;
- Overview of business operations;
- Preparation of reports or written materials and
- Health insurance forms and any other employee benefit items.

Independent of what your organization may provide in the way of orientation, you should develop your own orientation procedure including:

- introduction to co-workers
- taking the employee to a first day lunch
- providing background or project support reading material.

Finally, for a more complete orientation program you may also consider including the following elements as part of your program:

- Organizational history
- Discussion of medical and emergency services
- Holidays, time off and leave
- Facilities accessibility after hours and on weekends
- Safety procedures and precautions
- Promotion and transfer procedures
- Grievance Procedures

Some very progressive organizations go several steps further and send a welcome letter to the new employee's home, issue an introduction card to the new employee to wear for the first week on the job and have one of the top executives welcome the new employee again some time during the first week on the job.

A useful handbook developed by J. Clifton Lundberg, chief executive officer, Byvideo Inc., Sunnyvale, California, is capsulized below:

★ My primary goals are to "xyz." Your goals should be compatible with these.

★ Creativity. You do not get an "A" simply by solving all the problems within your jurisdiction. An integral part of your job is to identify new opportunities and recommend creative ways to take advantage of them.

★ Questions. It is your responsibility to understand the "rules" relating to your job—that is, how you succeed and how you fail. If anything of significance is unclear, you have an obligation to ask questions. Ignorance is no excuse.

★ Remembering. Through whatever method you find successful, you must remember items of importance or those requiring some sort of action. This includes requests made to you in writing as well as oral orders made in passing. If you can do this without writing, you have a better memory than I.

★ Overtime. Routine, substantial overtime is neither necessary nor desirable. On the other hand, almost any level of overtime is mandatory if that's what it takes to get a particular job done.

★ Your problems. I will try to be sensitive to your problems, but it is your specific responsibility to tell me about the important ones. I do not expect to have to draw them out of you.

★ Job offers and contacts with competitors. I expect you to look after your own personal interests, but I also expect to be informed of all discussions related to outside employment and all contacts with competitors.

★ Dress is important because it creates a perceived image with outsiders and it sets an example for others in the company. I expect professional consideration of both facts.

★ Surprises are bad, unless they are good. But even if they are good they should not be very big, because that would probably mean you should have known about them sooner.

The preceding items are important to me. They are intended to be fundamental enough so that they will be important to you also. If any of them are unclear or objectionable to you, please discuss them with me.

For your review, and to stimulate some ideas for developing your own system, here is a sample orientation checklist used by a major business machines manufacturer.

CHART 9
EMPLOYEE ORIENTATION PROCEDURE

☐ Sales   ☐ Systems   ☐ Field Engineering   ☐ Office

EMPLOYEE'S NAME_____ BRANCH_____

There are many Policies and Procedures that a New Employee is anxious to know and with which he should become acquainted during the first few days of his employment. The following list will assist in the covering of these points. A check provided in the space after each item will suffice to indicate that the item has been discussed with the New Employee.

INTRODUCTION   — To other members of Branch or Group — either
                    individually or at meeting, depending upon
                    size of organization.   ☐

BRANCH TOUR   — Location of various facilities, telephones,
                    mail, parking arrangements, and any other
                    local aspects.   ☐

CONFERENCE   — With District/Branch management to obtain
                    an understanding of the respective
                    departments and the relationship to the
                    employee's position.   ☐

CONTRACT REVIEW — Explain key points covered by his contract,
                    including salary and responsibilities.   ☐

COVERAGE OF PART 1

SECTION 1.1 —   ☐
     Information regarding the Company.

SECTION 1.2 —   ☐
     Employee privileges and benefits (Give employee booklets on
     group insurance, retirement plan, stock purchase plan and
     acquaint with availability of Employee's Credit
     Union.)

SECTION 1.3 —   ☐
     Employee responsibilities.

SECTION 1.4—
    Employee payroll plan, travel advances, deductions and expenses.

ALSO SUBJECT—
    1.4.1-8 — Branch hours

ITEMS TO BE SUBMITTED ON NEW HIRES:

_____ Personnel Action Notice

_____ Federal Withholding Tax (Form W-4)

_____ Application for Fidelity Bond

_____ Patent Agreement

_____ Conflict of Interest

_____ Employee Indoctrination

_____ Medical Examiners Report

_____ (Optional) Savings Bond Application

FOLLOWING INFORMATION TO BE COVERED WITH ALL EMPLOYEES

A. EMPLOYMENT INFORMATION

_____ Standard of Conduct

_____ Salary Administration

_____ Discuss Performance Reviews

_____ Explain Preparation and Use of Forms

_____ Outline Various Phases Of Training Program

_____ Reporting Of Absence Or Tardiness

_____ Safety Rules

_____ Promotional Opportunities Within Corporation

_____ Probationary Period

_____ Employee Suggestions & Complaints

B. DEPARTMENTAL INFORMATION

_____ 1. Technical Library (Systems & Sales only)
Acquaint with availability & proper use of Technical material in
library.

_____ 2. Set up and explain Form 1391 (Sales only)

_____ 3. Initiate & explain purpose of Form 1117 (Sales only)

_____ 4. Advertising and reference material file (Sales and Systems
Personnel)

_____ 5. Acquaint with qualification requirements for sales school
(Sales Only)

_____ 6. Business Ethics (Sales only)
Review of F.M.M. Subject 1.3.11

_____ 7. Distribute keys for desks or Branch Quarters for access to Branch
afterwork hours (Sales & Systems)

_____ 8. Dealer Program (Field Engineering only)
F.M.M. 2.10.15

C. BENEFITS

_____ A. Medical Coverage
    1. Hospitalization
    2. Surgery
    3. Out-Patient
_____ B. Major Medical Coverage
_____ C. Claims Procedure
_____ D. Disability Coverage
    1. Service Days (where applicable)
    2. Salary Continuation
    3. Weekly Disability
_____ E. Life Insurance
_____ F. Pension Plan
    1. Non-Contributory
    2. Contributory
_____ G. Educational Aid
_____ H. Stock Purchase
_____ I. Credit Union
_____ J. Authorized Absences
    1. Holidays
    2. Vacation
    3. Maternity/Military Leaves
    4. Disability Leaves
    5. Bereavement Leaves
    6. Jury Duty

7. Personal Leaves

_____ K. Savings Bond Enrollment

ALL EMPLOYEES

I have read and discussed the Corporation Policies and Procedures as outlined above — In particular the Manual Subject 1.3.1-4 on Private Dealings has been reviewed and is understood. I will, to the best of my ability, abide by these procedures and policies.

I understand that _____ is an Equal Opportunity Employer and that it is the policy of the Corporation to employ, promote and upgrade personnel on the basis of ability, experience, training and merit, without regard to race, creed, color, sex, age, ancestry or national origin.

Date	Employer's Signature

In addition to concurring in the above, I have also verified the Employee's birthdate to be

month	day	year

from the following source document _____

Date	Signature

Title

A Word About Probationary Periods

Despite thoroughness in the process of selecting new employees, it's wise to predicate the final decision to retain an employee based upon the successful completion of a probationary period. In a sense, both the employee and the company are "on trial" during the probationary period. Each is evaluating the other and forming impressions which will affect the final decision.

The best time to introduce new employees to the probationary period concept (not to be confused with being put "on probation" for inappropriate behavior or performance, Chapter 35) is during the initial interview. However, the nitty gritty explanation and initiation should take place just subsequent to or on the employee's first day. If the probationary period is spelled out as part of the customary orientation procedure, then everything generally runs smoothly.

Regardless of its length, a probationary period offers a chance to observe new workers on the job. Regular observations should be made; you should meet frequently with new employees to discuss progress, answer questions, and provide an extra dose of supervision.

When it's time to make a final decision, compare observed performance with the job requirements as reflected on the job descriptions (which, of course, were mutually formulated). If there is any doubt about the employee's ability to do the job, he or she should not be retained. This decision should be arrived at objectively, and discussed tactfully with employees. When unsuitable employees are retained, a disservice is done to them as well as to the department and company as a whole. The mere presence of poor employees can help to cause morale problems for the good employees, and affect the department's and the company's overall efficiency.

Here's a checklist for handling probationary periods:

- ☐ **introduce the policy early** in the interview process
- ☐ institute the policy on the **first day**
- ☐ **meet frequently** to help the new employee
- ☐ **compare observed performance** with job requirements
- ☐ **do not retain** unsuitable employees.

A Word on Employee Contracts

Increasingly, mid to upper level employees are requesting an employee contract before coming on board with your organization. Surprisingly, employee contracts often work to your advantage rather than the employee's. They are useful when there is a pronounced need to elaborate on the employee's assigned tasks and duties, if you need to protect trade secrets or inventions, and if you need to limit competition from the employee should he or she depart and go into business for himself. The employee contract can also be looked upon as a marketing tool—it aids in attracting top achievers who have well-developed skills in looking out for themselves.

The checklist below summarizes the essential elements of an employee contract from the employer's side:

- ☐ Use an attorney to draw up or review the agreement.
- ☐ Produce a contract that is in harmony with existing corporate policies and procedures.
- ☐ Use terminology that does not appear overly restrictive to the employee, especially in the case of his or her departure.
- ☐ Spell out the exact responsibilities and duties of the employee, and the benefits and prerequisites that you are responsible for providing.
- ☐ Offer the contract in unison with or subsequent to your letter offering employment.
- ☐ Discuss with the job applicant the exact provisions of the contract and all of the ramifications.
- ☐ Seek mediation in the event of contractual disputes.
- ☐ Inform the employee of provisions which prevail in the event of his or her departure.

While there are many advantages to using employment contracts, one major disadvantage is that in case of dispute, the courts generally side in favor of employees. Moreover, it is difficult to dislodge an employee with an employment contract who is not living up to the contract, without a well-developed case against him or her.

The Eleven Rules of Contracts

CHART 10

The *Small Business Report,* Monteray, CA, suggests that the following provisions should be included in employment contracts:

1. All parties covered must be clearly identified.
2. Terms of the agreement: Three to five years is the most common time span.
3. The job position: The title of the job and a full description of responsibilities.
4. Salary/Compensation: The basic salary and when and how it will be reviewed.
5. Annual bonus: How a bonus is earned and what form it will take—stock, cash, etc.
6. Long-term incentive rewards: How earned, the method of calculation, the means of evaluation and the time period. The actual compensation method is also agreed to in advance.

7. Employee benefits: All non-cash benefits are explained. This would include insurance, health, company cars, vacations, and profit sharing.

8. Termination agreements: All reasonable contingencies should be covered. These include:

   Death—salary continues to a named beneficiary for a certain period of time.

   Disability—compensation, if any, in excess of the employee benefit package.

   Termination with cause—requires serious misconduct, not merely poor performance. All salary and benefits would cease.

   Termination without cause—covers a situation where the employee and the company may wish to severe their relationship even though there is no misconduct on either side. An example would be a senior executive disagreeing with the board over the company's goals.

   Voluntary termination—covers the employee leaving voluntarily and with permission.

   Golden parachute—covers senior management compensation in the event a hostile takeover or proxy fight results in a change of corporate strategy.

9. Non-compete provision: This clause must first fully define the firm's business and then specify the geographic area and time frame in which the employee cannot compete with the business.

10. Confidentiality provision: Prohibits employees from disclosing defined company secrets or using proprietary information to recruit employees.

11. Arbitration agreement: To avoid costly litigation, include this provision which waives court enforcement in favor of a defined arbitration procedure. The employer, however, should retain the right to seek an injunction in competition or trade secret disputes.

If the candidate you've selected for the job seeks an employment contract, it's certainly not a reason to balk. Handled properly, the contract can help solidify the working arrangement and produce a win-win situation. It is also possible to make the contract contingent upon successful completion upon the probationary period, thereby affording you ample protection against nonperformance.

In Section II, starting on page 70, the focus shifts to managing for increased productivity.

SECTION II

SCHEDULING FOR PRODUCTIVITY

Productivity is a difficult concept to define. The term productivity is often bantered about, yet few comprehend its meaning. Industry studies consistently fail to acknowledge the complex effect of multiple inputs and outputs on productivity. In the early 70's, Bela Gold, of Case Western Reserve University observed, "even casual examination of modern industries demonstrated that output per person-hour measures neither the efficiency of production operations as a whole nor the efficiency of labor's own efforts."

In this book the term productivity will be used to mean systematic efforts to increase, extend, or achieve human and organizational benefit outputs and decrease resource inputs. This definition represents an adaptation of work done by noted productivity expert and author Robert R. Carkhuff.

In your role as supervisor you may be required to integrate many elements—human resources, raw materials, supplies, plant and equipment, all within a variety of technical and organizational constraints. The interplay of all of these is usually needed to achieve an end product, but the effective use and supervision of human resources, your staff, is generally your most important responsibility.

Chapters 9 through 15, comprising Section II, focus on how best to harness natural work patterns and thus schedule the work flow for improved productivity, while sparing you of productivity terminology claptrap. This section will be of particular importance to you if you are often unable to account for your staff's periods of low output.

CHAPTER NINE

MANAGING THROUGH
THE SEASONS

Every good supervisor or manager quickly learns that employee output, motivation and overall attitude towards work is significantly influenced by the seasons. Your staff feels the same as you do about the first fabulous day of spring when the last possible trace of winter has passed, and the smell of chlorophyll replaces wintergreen. Let's roll through the year on a monthly basis and examine what the supervisor is likely to experience or observe.

After reading this chapter, the answer to the questions will be clear:

☐ What period of time known as one of **mass depression** becomes one of moderate productivity as employees seek fulfillment through work?
☐ What are the **two highest energy level periods** of the year?
☐ Why is "**Spring fever**" nothing to worry about?
☐ Does August represent the **productivity "pits"**?
☐ What are other **peak performance periods** during the year and holiday season?

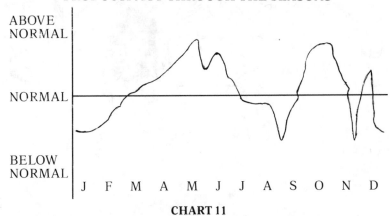

PRODUCTIVITY THROUGH THE SEASONS

CHART 11

71

January and February

A week or two after the holidays, during the dead of winter many employees begin to get depressed. With fewer daylight hours, most employees are commuting to and from the office in the dark and feel that they're "missing the day." A few blizzards or snow storms in February, very rough traveling and the feeling of being stranded contribute to the depressed feeling of many. It is during this time, however, that many employees display great productivity as they look to their jobs as a source of activity and fulfillment.

March and April

In most parts of the country, spring has still not arrived in March. Moreover, March with its variable weather pattern: a warm day here, snow storm the next day, howling winds or rains another day, can actually be more disruptive than January or February. By the end of March, with daylight hours steadily increasing, spirits begin to pick up and with some sporadic days of sunshine in April increasing energy levels can occur. By the end of April, and heading into May, many employees are super charged, maintaining one of their highest energy levels of the entire year.

May and June

As days of sparkling sunshine ensue, employees' rising energy levels which had been directed towards their jobs are often re-

focussed to "Spring clean up" and outdoor activities. Many a supervisor has felt the decline in output of his/her staff as the flowers bloom or when the first real beach weekend occurs.

The reduction of attention span and decline in overall productivity remains for several weeks in mid May and throughout most of June until sunshine-filled days have become the standard. Then employees adjust to and accept the summer and renew efforts on the job, or the humidity comes and everyone is happy to be busy at work in the (hopefully) streamlined air-conditioned office.

July and August

Surprisingly, these months do not represent the pits of productivity that many first-time supervisors had originally feared. To be sure, many people take their vacations during this time and this can be somewhat disruptive to operations. But July and the dog days of August can indeed be times of reasonable output.

The end of August, however, is a different story. Many employees seem to be in a holding pattern of rather low productivity which is miraculously cured directly after Labor Day.

September, October Through Mid-November

As the kids go back to school, the humidity breaks and chill returns to the night air, employees once again become highly energized. September, after Labor Day through mid-November often represents the period of greatest productivity and a time in which new challenges and new major projects can be undertaken.

The Federal Government and many major corporations begin their new fiscal year on October 1st. The Fall (and Spring) is often a time of new hiring. Many new supervisors wish that Autumn could last all year long.

Mid-November Through December

This six to seven week period at the end of the year broken up by holidays, longer week-ends or vacation time is not the total productivity disaster that many supervisors fear. Leading up to Thanksgiving many employees are capable of great accomplishment. Following the Thanksgiving vacation through mid-December can indeed be a time of high energy for your staff.

Approaching Christmas, however, one can readily notice a drop off in output as much attention is focused on how they plan shopping or travel. The annual office Christmas party plus a slew of other parties and activities throughout December can contribute to a general sluggishness in overall effort. The turkey, wine, cookies and egg nog tend to leave everyone a little heavier, a little slower and a little less productive. Many supervisors "write-off" the last half of December as a total loss, though this is a good period for instilling company spirit, staff and departmental meetings and maintenance activities.

Supervising or managing through the seasons requires a little foresight, empathy and experience. While it would be nice from a scheduling standpoint to have balanced output throughout the year, philosophically, at least, the workplace is a more interesting place because of the holidays and the seasons.

Here's a checklist of key points presented in the chapter:

- [ ] January—**low output** improving towards month's end
- [ ] February—**continued rise**, still below normal
- [ ] March—**increasing output, interrupted** by weather problems
- [ ] April—**increasing output**, climbing toward spring peak
- [ ] May—**productivity peak**, followed by spring fever drop-off
- [ ] June—**reasonable productivity** following adjustment to summer
- [ ] July—**declining productivity**, but air conditioning salvages many
- [ ] August—**declining output**, heightened by vacations and anticipation of autumn
- [ ] September—**resurgence** following Labor Day
- [ ] October—**strong productivity** month (although Indian Summer can cause a downward flip)
- [ ] November—**declining** output approaching Turkey Day
- [ ] December—some gains early in month, **a wipe out** thereafter

In Chapter Ten which follows, let's look at how good employees internally program their own cycle of productivity.

CHAPTER TEN

SUPERVISING CYCLES OF PRODUCTIVITY

Linda won't transcribe tapes late in the day or anytime on Friday. As a matter of fact, she has established a personal work pattern or cycle in which specific tasks will be undertaken throughout the course of the week.

Susan, the production supervisor, rarely interferes with Linda's cycle unless an urgent report or letter must be completed. Is Linda an obstinate employee, undermining production needs of her office? Is Susan deficient as a production supervisor? For the surprising answer to these questions plus the ones below, flip the page.

- ☐ What is a **personal cycle** of productivity?
- ☐ How can the supervisor best **take advantage** of good employees cycles?
- ☐ What **benefits** accrue to acknowledging good employees' cycles?
- ☐ What are ways to **get the most** out of productive employees?
- ☐ How does an **office crisis** affect an employee's cycle?
- ☐ Do **supervisors have cycles** of productivity?

Recognizing the Cycle

Returning to the scenario of Susan and Linda, is either woman derelict in her duties?

For either woman, quite the contrary. Linda is an exceptionally effective member of the production staff, and Susan directs the production department skillfully. Linda has long since determined her productive peaks and valleys throughout the course of the normal work week, and hence, recognizes her personal **cycle of**

productivity. For all but urgent assignments, Susan acknowledges Linda's ability to maintain high productivity by handling assignments on those days and at those hours which achieve a relatively constant "effort to task" ratio.

Roberta, Linda's equally efficient production staff partner, also maintains high productivity by personally prioritizing assignments. While Linda and Roberta have similar production responsibilities, each has different strengths and weaknesses, varying energy levels (throughout the work week), and has long since gauged these factors so that each knows what can best be undertaken when.

Employees Establish Their Cycles

Good employees should be afforded the opportunity to establish their personal productivity cycles, and within reason, they should be allowed to undertake assignments in a manner which best suits them. So many employees devise countless ways to diminish personal productivity by stretching out assignments, or by coasting until checkout time. However, highly productive employees such as Linda, Roberta and Susan take pride in consistently maintaining high productivity. Enabling them to respond based upon personal cycles of productivity results in high job satisfaction and yields a greater long-range output.

Another reason to let productive people follow their own schedules is that they will be less fatigued. It is quite draining to continually be meeting often arbitrary deadlines or to undertake selected tasks when one does not feel fully equipped to do so. Productive employees, allowed to pace themselves, can accomplish more and remain more vibrant.

How to Get the Most Out of Productive Employees

Productive employees may have an **internal "time grid"** that charts their cycle of productivity. Quite often, no formal sketch or chart is ever made. Nevertheless, it does exist. Productive employees may also be leery of telling supervisors that they'd "rather not handle the DEF report right now" because they "can do a better job on it tomorrow morning," and the "GHI assignment could be better undertaken now."

Independent of discussion, there are four basic ways to get the most from productive employees in cognizance of cycles of productivity.

77

1) **Provide enough and varied assignments so the cycle can be used.** If an employee only has one assignment then, obviously, there is little leeway in undertaking the assignment at the most personally opportune time. With numerous assignments, a productive employee can strategically arrange his/her schedule.

2) **Be flexible in "due" dates when possible.** Productive employees will finish the important jobs on time. Assignments of lesser importance will be finished as soon as possible. The more flexibility a productive employee is given in completing assignments, the greater the opportunity for him/her to execute assignments in accordance with the cycle. More often than not, given flexible due dates, the productive employee will complete many assignments sooner than you anticipated.

3) **Avoid late afternoon and surprise assignments**. The productive employee, in concurrence with his/her cycle of productivity, intuitively allocates tasks for the late afternoon. (For an extended view of the harm in issuing late afternoon assignments, see Chapter 26.)

4) Closely related to the above, **always try to provide advance notice of assignments to productive employees so that sufficient time is available to schedule the new assignment in accordance with the cycle of productivity**. If you usually provide flexible due dates, then the need for advanced notice is not essential.

Reprogramming the Cycle

The cycle of productivity of a good worker can be reprogrammed to meet the needs of the organization, company or department. For example, if an important report must be finished within four days, good employees will prepare themselves and will generate the requisite energy to successfully accomplish the task. In the short run, good employees can reprogram their cycles of productivity to handle a crisis.

However, forcing a good worker to reprogram his or her cycle for an extended period is not recommended. Since he or she is already highly efficient, an extended variation soon becomes an imposition, and can upset the delicate balance by which the productive employee remains productive.

Supervisors and managers have cycles of productivity too. After all, you chose to read this chapter at **this** particular time, didn't you?

Here's a brief checklist for supervising cycles of productivity:

- [ ] Let good **employees establish** and follow their cycles.
- [ ] **Provide enough assignments so the cycle can be effectively used.**
- [ ] **Be flexible as to due dates (when possible).**
- [ ] **Avoid** late afternoon and surprise assignments.
- [ ] **Give advance notice** of assignments (when possible).
- [ ] **Avoid forcing reprogramming** of a cycle for an extended period.
- [ ] **Recognize your own cycle** and work with it!

In the next chapter we'll discuss how the effective supervisor streamlines his/her own schedule.

CHAPTER ELEVEN
STREAMLINING YOUR ACT

In order to supervise others effectively and schedule their tasks and activities, it's necessary that you're able to schedule effectively your own tasks and activities first. Streamlining your act means being able to set goals and maintain personal time management.

The supervisor who's always changing course, or chasing the clock will have a difficult time effectively scheduling the staff. By "streamlining your act" you establish a model of which employees may emulate, and increase the quality of the time that you put into the job.

This chapter will help you to answer the following questions:

□ When goal setting, why is it useful to first over pick the goals you'd like to accomplish?
□ What is meant by ready, fire, aim?
□ How does establishing files in advance enhance personal time management?
□ What is meant by multiple stations?
□ What are some techniques for "creating" time?
□ What is the single greatest time saver?

The Magic of Goal Setting

In 1954, the graduating class of Yale University was polled to determine what percentage of the class had established written financial goals. Some 86% of the class had established no goals whatsoever, while 11% had established some sort of goals but had either not written them down or could not produce them if requested and only 3% had clearly established well-defined, written financial goals.

In 1974, a follow-up study was done on Yale's 1954 graduating class. To the amazement of those conducting the study, the 3% who in 1954 had clearly established well defined written goals, now had a combined net worth that exceeded the other 97% of the graduating class, combined! Undoubtedly, you have read or heard of the importance of setting goals. While we all maintain some notion of where we wish to head, the goal setting process is often shortchanged.

Here are some tips on goal-setting that help to greatly simplify the process:

☐ Over pick—When choosing goals that you wish to accomplish as a supervisor on the job and for your own career, initially, over pick. After listing all of the things you'd like to accomplish go back and realistically assess those that are of top priority versus those that are nice but, on second inspection, not that important.

☐ Remember "Less is More"—A few well-chosen goals that are challenging, yet reachable are preferablewhen making your selection. It is of no value to anyone to choose unrealistic, unreachable goals that only lead to frustration and despair.

☐ Reduce "interruptions" or "noise." Once you've chosen challenging, but reachable goals, tune out all other distractions. You reach a goal that much sooner and are better prepared to establish new goals as time and resources permit.

☐ Post your goals—Many successful supervisors and managers have had their goals typed up, then reduced and laminated, or photocopied and distributed for convenient and frequent review. The easiest way to stay on target is to periodically review the goals you've established, daily if necessary, so as to remain in a highly focused, on-target mode. When you and your staff are operating in such a manner, great results can be accomplished.

☐ Build in flexibility—While it's important to establish a few well chosen goals, recognize that the nature of your responsibilities and tasks often change and a goal that was necessary and appropriate yesterday may suddenly no longer be valid. While remaining steadfast and on-target in pursuit of your goals, also objectively assess them to determine their present and continuing applicability. The ability to change or shift with your organization or department's needs is as important as your ability to select appropriate goals.

Ready, Fire, Aim

Peters and Waterman, authors of *In Search of Excellence*, observed that for too many years American businesses were stuck in the "ready, aim, fire" mode—in order to get ready to undertake a project, reams of study, analysis, assessment and evaluation were first undertaken, followed by careful planning, test marketing, or simulation and then firing—finally diving head-long into the project or market area.

The "ready, fire, aim" concept which can readily be used on a project level involves making a brief evaluation or assessment of the task at hand, followed by an early "firing" involving getting into the actual project activity even if on a piecemeal or limited basis, and then "aiming" which involves readjusting, modifying or honing project plans. The "ready, fire, aim" concept is useful and important to supervisors because it effectively shortens the time in which full-scale project activities can be initiated while minimizing the risk of misfiring or misallocating resources. If you are operating on a limited budget, (and, who isn't?) then the "ready, fire, aim" concept may well be a necessity.

Establishing Milestones

Establishing milestones for the realization or completion of the goals you've chosen is essential for successful supervision. Normally the time period that you have to accomplish goals is a given to the situation—deadlines have been imposed from above or from the marketplace.

Preparing a milestone chart is an easy way to maintain command of the timing and progress toward established goals. A simple milestone chart such as that presented on the following page can be prepared which delineates each task and subtask including starting time, ending time and a schedule of delivery of products. There are numerous software applications that can be used in preparing milestone charts.

The calendar block back method assures that a goal will be achieved and milestones reached by using the monthly calendar. Here's how it works. Start from the due date or deadline for which a task, project or deliverable must be completed. Then plot the subtasks and activities that must be undertaken from that due date to the present day. In other words, proceed in reverse using the monthly calendar to establish realistic, interim dates that reflect organizational resources, staff vacation time, holidays, week-ends and other down time and which reflect reasonable output levels.

By using the calendar block back method, you can quickly determine that if, for example, subtask two in pursuit of goal X was accomplished two days late, then the whole project will be two days late unless immediate corrective action is taken.

One exceptionally effective supervisor used to schedule projects to be finished a full week before the actual deadline by treating the artificial deadline as real. In this way the supervisor always finished projects on time or early.

Michael LeBoeuf, Ph.D., in his book, *Working Smart*, points out that as a scheduling rule of thumb, estimate how much time you think a given activity or task will take and multiply it by 1.25. If the task is something that's never been undertaken before,

MILESTONE CHART

SUBTASK	AUG.	SEPT.	OCT.	NOV.
PREPARE BIBLIOGRAPHY				
A. Compile list				
B. Analyze list				
C. Prepare list				
D. Prepare camera-ready				
E. Submit				27
PREPARE SUPPLEMENTARY MATERIAL				
A. Determine need				
B. Make rec.			28	
C. Draft copy				
D. Develop graphics				
E. Prepare camera-ready				
F. Submit				29
PREPARE RECOMMENDATIONS				
A. Determine need				
B. Prepare report				
C. Submit				30

MILESTONE KEY

Milestone	Project Date	Comment	Actual Completion Date
27. Submit Bibliography	10/29		
28. Make Rec.	9/21		
29. Submit Sup.	10/29		
30. Submit Recs.	11/8		

CHART 12

83

CALENDAR BLOCK BACK

MONTH ___ MARCH ___   YEAR ___

SUNDAY	MONDAY	TUESDAY	WEDNESDAY	THURSDAY	FRIDAY	SATURDAY
	1 Submitted Feb. 24	2 Deliver draft workshop planning report	3	4	5	6
7	8	9 Submitted to typing	10	11	12	13
14	15 Assessment of conf. capabilities Deliver profile revisions	16	17	18	19 Assessment of target audience. 52 pages Deliver	20
21	22	23	24	25	26	27
28	29	30	31 Deliver final workshop planning report			

CHART 13

multiply the time you think it will take by 1.5. A common weakness among capable people is that they sometimes unrealistically estimate the time it will take to accomplish something. By adding a small safety margin, the probability of assembling the requisite resources and finishing the project on time increases.

Insiders' Tips

Here are some other suggestions, which I have found to work very well, for augmenting your personal schedule, First, recognize that establishing files in advance, taking the time to get organized, and assembling the necessary resources to undertake a project may not seem like whirl-wind activities, yet greatly contribute to your overall project effort.

Another technique is the use of multiple stations. An example will help illustrate. If you wear contact lenses, you know that it makes sense to keep extra saline solution and storage tubs in your desk at work, at home, in your car and in your locker at the gym. In this way you're always prepared without having to carry these materials on your person.

So it is with supervision.

The resources you may choose to post at multiple stations may include pens, note pads, calculators, etc. If you use these items enough and the need may occur at any of several locations, free yourself from having to carry them by setting up stations in advance.

As any good supervisor knows, one of the best ways to save time is to delegate. Even better is to not do a task—by that I mean any task or activity that can safely be eliminated, should be eliminated.

You can also "create" time by imagining you've been assigned to undertake a project on your own say, every Tuesday morning from 9 to 11. The project is to run 15 weeks and you must do it alone, undisturbed. Now that you've cleared away the next 15 Tuesdays from 9 to 11 in the morning, sit back and relax since there really is no project of this nature assigned to you. However, with this mental framework and some self-discipline you can maintain two free hours every Tuesday morning for a 15-week period.

Here's a checklist for streamlining your act:

☐ Remember the magic of **goal setting**, and set your goals now.
☐ **Over pick the goals** you wish to accomplish, prioritize them and start on the important ones.

- ☐ **Eliminate** distractions, interruptions, noise!
- ☐ **Post** your **goals**.
- ☐ Build **flexibility** into your schedule.
- ☐ Use the **ready, fire, aim** method.
- ☐ **Establish milestones** and a milestones chart.
- ☐ Use **calendar block back** to ensure that deadlines will be met.
- ☐ **Multiply** how much time you think a task will take **by 1.25**.
- ☐ **Establish files** and get organized in advance.
- ☐ Use **multiple stations** so that you can carry less.
- ☐ **Delegate**.
- ☐ **Eliminate** what can be eliminated.
- ☐ **Create time** by assuming an imaginary assignment.

Now let's take a look at some of the ways your staff engages in non-productive activity—favorite employee time wasters.

CHAPTER TWELVE

FAVORITE EMPLOYEE TIME WASTERS

In addition to serving in the role for which they are employed, a number of other activities capture the time of employees during business hours. On the pages that follow is a review of favorite employee time wasters: those events, behaviors, and phenomena that infringe upon the output and effectiveness of an organization, company, department or division. While isolated incidences may not in themselves have a sizeable effect on overall company performance, repetitive occurrence by numerous employees will indeed have a pronounced effect.

It's not likely that any of the time wasters to be discussed will be news to you. At one time or another you've probably engaged in a few of them yourself. From the perspective of management and supervision, however, it will be useful to examine employees favorite time wasting activities anew.

This chapter provides the answers to these questions:

- ☐ How costly can "coasting" until check-out time be?
- ☐ Can one be over-organized?
- ☐ How can employees take two lunch breaks on the same day?
- ☐ Is waiting for paychecks a time waster?
- ☐ Why must timesheets be filled out on a continuing basis rather than once per week?
- ☐ What are five ways the "plastered" employee causes harm?

Coasting Until Check-out Time

Many employees in ending their work day have a tendency to quit work 15 to 30 minutes in advance and coast until check-out time. While it is not possible for everyone to remain productive during the closing minutes of each day, if the phenomenon of coasting until check-out time is widespread within a department, or throughout an entire company, the net loss can be staggering.

As an illustration, if 45 employees out of a total of 450, habitually coast for the last 30 minutes of each day, and if the average wage is $10 per hour, during one month containing twenty workdays, the company will pay $4,500 for non-productive time. Adding benefits and other costs incurred yields a figure of over $5,600. On a yearly basis their figure rises to over $67,000:

45 employees X $10.00/hr. X 30 minutes/day X 20 days = $4,500
$4,500/month X 1.25 (for benefits) X 12 months = $67,500

If the time spent "coasting" is used to plan the next working day or to make mental preparations for future tasks, then this

time utilization becomes productive. However, if many employees use their last 15 or 30 minutes of each day to merely observe the clock and wait until its hands finally reach their departure hour, then a major problem exists.

Clock watching may also occur prior to the lunch hour. Many employees coast for 15 to 20 minutes before lunch, as well as prior to coffee breaks, department meetings and other planned events.

Organization and Reorganizations

Another favorite time waster is the continual organization and reorganization of desks, files, shelves, etc. One's working materials can only be organized so many times before a state of diminishing returns is reached, after which time there is **no** utility in continuing. As a general rule, if someone is able to extract needed information from desks or files within a minute or two, then he/she is sufficiently organized. Any further time invested in the organization or reorganization of materials is a waste of time.

Secretaries and clerical workers often avoid typing or other tasks in favor of activities that they perceive as being easier or less tedious, such as filing or labeling. Those employees that use the last 15 to 30 minutes of the day to organize themselves for the next day, so that they may start fresh on new projects or resume with renewed vigor are, however, making good time utilization. (See Chapter Thirteen, "Using Friday Afternoons Profitably")

Moreover, it is recommended that employees take a few minutes at the end of each day and each week to prepare for the coming day or week. Thus, it is possible that an employee may appear to be "coasting" until check-out time, or to be organizing or over-organizing, while they are actually engaging in a useful and productive period.

Carefully Reading Junk Mail

The mail order houses, national manufacturers and distributors, and business and professional services groups all use the mail to build business. Any employee who has been with an organization for longer than three months is bound to receive a steady stream of junk mail as his/her name is added to an ever growing number of mailing lists. An employee may receive five to ten pieces of unsolicited mail per day. When this occurs, it is important for the employee to judge accurately what should be read and acted upon, what should be filed for future use, and what should be discarded immediately. Unfortunately, many employees take delight in reading every piece of information that has been sent to them and use the reviewing of mail as a procrastination technique.

Charles Shearin, Ph.D., president of Vicore, Inc. which offers several excellent human resource development programs, reports that he frequently stacks his mail in piles based on the apparent urgency of the communication. Much of the non-urgent (particularly third class) mail is ultimately never opened!

It is nearly impossible to legislate how mail should be circulated to employees. Holding the mail until an hour late in the day is not recommended because an employee may need a vital piece of information.

One way to reduce the amount of junk mail sent to your office is to contact the Direct Marketing Association and request that certain individuals be removed from master mailing lists used by association members (Mail Preference Service, Direct Marketing Association, 6 E. 43rd St., New York, NY 10017.) Another way to reduce the flow of miscellaneous mail to employees, is to instruct the receiving secretary to direct several similar packages to the head of the department, who can then make a decision regarding who else should be informed of the correspondence.

Taking Two Lunch Breaks

This technique has been widely practiced particularly in job-shop and factory settings where an employee may easily sneak behind machinery or other shelter and munch his/her sandwich prior to the designated lunch hour. When the designated lunch hour arrives, the employee has created "time" beyond that previously taken while devouring lunch.

This practice is unfair to the company. In a factory setting, it is potentially dangerous. Within an office setting, spills and food stains often end up on company documents and paper work which diminishes the professionalism of the entire office. Unless there is a designated area within your organization where an employee may have refreshment, and other than during designated coffee or meal breaks, **employees should be discouraged from consuming food at work stations**.

Related to eating lunch before the designated time is the occurrence of employees bringing breakfast to work. It is often difficult for an employee to eat breakfast before departing for work, particularly in an urban setting where one has to fight morning traffic. However, allowing employees to bring breakfast into work produces the following harmful side effects:

- ★ The amount of time that the employee spends eating breakfast is, of course, non-productive time to the company;
- ★ Those employees that have adequately planned their day and ate breakfast before departing for work are, in essence, penalized;
- ★ The potential for soiling papers or other company owned equipment is high; and
- ★ The practice detracts from the professionalism of the entire organization.

Waiting for Pay Checks

An all-time favorite employee time waster is waiting for the pay check. Whether pay checks are delivered on Fridays, bi-weekly or monthly, most employees are keenly aware of pay day. If the time of the day at which the pay check arrives varies, many employees will shuffle through the day waiting until the check actually arrives and then make a mad dash to the bank for a deposit. Others may have anxiety about the check not coming or containing an incorrect total.

The best policy in fighting this time waster is to distribute the checks at the **same time** each pay day. Thus, it will be known throughout the company that checks will be delivered exactly at 1:30 a.m., and employees can make plans accordingly. It might be wise to issue checks immediately on pay day so that employees may receive their check, take care of personal responsibilities, and get back to work. Distributing pay checks early in the day also affords the advantage of reducing the time that employees waste precalculating the figures that the check should contain or being anxious as to what the amount will be.

Excessive, Elaborate Travel Arrangements

Often when an employee has to travel, he or she has the tendency to spend more time on travel plans than is necessary. For example, when an employee has to travel for business reasons, particularly to an area that is near resort facilities, there is a tendency for additional time to be wasted beyond that of normal pre-trip banter, discussing the trip.

One way to eliminate time frittered away on travel plans is to have a clerical or support person complete all travel arrangements including the itinerary, and submit a comprehensive package to the employee who has been authorized to travel. At the very least, this will eliminate some of the questions and conjecture as to where one will stay, when one will be arriving, and so forth.

Extensive Review of Timesheets

In nearly all organizations some type of timesheet or weekly reporting log must be completed and submitted to management. If this time sheet or log has been compiled on a daily basis, when Friday or the end of the recording period rolls around, there will be relatively little to do to complete the form.

However, if an employee does not enter the required data on a daily, or at least regular basis, at the end of the reporting period an extensive compilation and review of the timesheet or log will be necessary. The fact is that the time expended in trying to complete a timesheet a week later is far in excess of the time required to record information daily. Thus, employees should be instructed to **maintain timesheets or logs on a daily or regular basis**.

Getting Plastered on Friday Afternoons

A large number of employees, particularly in downtown office environments, think nothing of getting plastered in a local tavern on a Friday afternoon during the lunch hour. (Note: some prefer to get stoned.) Often, what should have been sixty minutes or less turns into two hours and more, and the employee's productivity for the rest of the day is virtually nil. What's worse, some decide to "celebrate" the end of the week as early as Thursday afternoon, and use the Thursday lunch period, as well as Friday, to get plastered.

This favorite employee time waster can only continue to flourish in the absence of good supervision. While it is common to conduct a farewell lunch for a departing employee, have a holiday celebration, or hold a staff luncheon following a good monthly or quarterly effort, if a sufficient number of employees get plastered every other Friday, significant costs to the company are incurred. Other liabilities to the company that accrue when employees get plastered on Friday include the following:

☐ The productivity of the employee is low;
☐ The employee's judgment and decision-making capabilities are diminished;
☐ The employee may not be able to adequately represent the company with on-site visitors or over the telephone;
☐ The hard-working, non-imbibing employee may be resentful; and
☐ The professionalism of the organization has been diminished.

There are many other time wasters. The supervisor who is at least aware of some traditional time wasters will be able to more readily acknowledge when they are occurring, and be able to diminish their effect.

Here's a checklist of favorite employee time wasters. Read it to your staff and convey the message that all such behaviors are to be eliminated:

- ☐ **Coasting** until checkout time
- ☐ **Over organizing**
- ☐ **Reading** junk mail carefully
- ☐ **Taking** two lunch breaks
- ☐ **Waiting** for paychecks
- ☐ **Making** excessive travel plans
- ☐ **Completing** time sheets once per week
- ☐ **Getting** plastered at lunch

In Chapter 13, "Using Friday Afternoon Profitably," we'll explore effective ways to combat some of the time wasters.

CHAPTER THIRTEEN

USING FRIDAY AFTERNOONS PROFITABLY

Late one Friday afternoon Bill Halloran walked past several offices of employees whom he supervised and noticed that about half didn't seem to be working. Many were on the telephone conducting casual conversations, apparently with friends or spouses; others were milling about, idly chattering or absorbed in some minor activity.

This didn't upset Bill because he realized that as the week-end approached it seemed nearly impossible for any supervisor to maintain a staff of fully alert and productive employees. Moreover, it is human nature to dwell upon that which we will be doing once the work day or work week has ended.

In this chapter we'll explore what can be done during seemingly "low productivity periods" and answer the questions:

- ☐ How can Bill's own **attitude** affect operations?
- ☐ Is **filing** a worthwhile activity late in the day?
- ☐ Is it all right for Bill to **meet with the staff** for an after work drink?
- ☐ How can Bill **better prepare staff** for the following week?
- ☐ What does an **open door policy** encourage?

Several weeks passed and Bill, an excellent supervisor, wondered if there weren't some ways to increase productivity on Friday afternoons while not appearing authoritarian or causing resentment and demoralizing his staff. After a while, Bill concluded that there were ways to accomplish his goal and that the best method for achieving the desired results was to develop a low-key, informal strategy to favorably guide the staff.

File, File, File

First Bill individually suggested to several employees that late Friday afternoon was a good time to make sure that personal and common files were in order, purged of unnecessary documents and properly catalogued or indexed. Bill's company was generally interested in reducing paper handling, and Friday afternoon was a particularly good time to reduce paper files when the material was available on disk or other ADP medium.

Bill also suggested that insurance and medical forms and miscellaneous correspondence be handled on Friday afternoons. The rationale for this suggestion is clear—filling out forms is largely routine work which does not require heavy thinking and thus is a suitable activity during the time in which employees are most distracted.

The Open Door

Without telling anyone, but making it rather obvious, Bill made available the last two hours of his Friday to any of his staff that wished to speak with him. Bill found that as the week drew to

a close his staff was much more likely to open up and discuss problems or, perhaps, offer new suggestions to improve operations.

As the weeks went by, Bill often was able to speak to as many as three or four of his staff, individually, late on Friday. Bill also encouraged project supervisors to meet informally with team members so that everyone could be off and running next Monday morning.

An Occasional Social Hour

Now and then somebody in Bill's staff decided to get a group together after work to partake of the Happy Hour at the nearby pub. Bill was frequently asked if he would attend such occasions and usually said yes. He did this for two reasons: one is, he genuinely liked his staff and liked to socialize with them for an hour or so on occasion after work; and two, he recognized that staff morale and productivity was generally higher on those Fridays in which it was known staff members would be meeting after work for a drink. Thus Bill supported this social venture, left his title back in the office, and became one of the gang.

Mixing Lower and Higher Priority Tasks

Bill recognized that initiating new tasks late in the afternoon, particularly on Friday afternoon, was never well received and generally represented bad policy. However, he did hit upon the idea of occasionally requesting selected staff members to undertake a small task which later would support a more important project. For example, he asked Al Flumen to outline the steps that would be necessary to solve a particular company problem.

The outline needed to be only one or two pages. Al did a good job on this seemingly lower priority task. Next Monday Bill assigned Al the job of writing a formal report based on the outline and heading up a team which would implement the suggestions and recommendations made. In asking Al to prepare the outline Bill neither requested a deadline or formally assigned the task to Al. Bill was merely seeking to obtain some good ideas for solving the problem and had a hunch that Al could be productively engaged even late Friday afternoon.

Attitude Adjustment

Finally, and perhaps most importantly, Bill realized that his own attitude regarding productivity late on Friday afternoon and the manner in which he pursued his tasks during this time period would heavily influence his staff. Bill knew of other supervisors who had largely given in to the TGIF syndrome as early as 3 p.m. He resolved that it was necessary not to let down his guard and exhibit de facto acceptance of sluffing off towards the week-end. In this way Bill was most effectively able to influence his employees to maintain a solid work effort.

In using late afternoons profitably, here's a checklist for future reference:

☐ Use a low key **informal strategy**
☐ Encourage employees to **file materials** or complete miscellaneous forms and correspondence
☐ Initiate an **open door policy**
☐ **Join the staff** for an occasional social hour
☐ **Initiate future tasks** as a creative exercise
☐ **Plan** next week's schedule
☐ Maintain your proper **attitude**: Lead by example.

Is there a way to let your staff work flexible hours while not disrupting your scheduling? Yes. Chapter 14 explores alternative work schedules.

CHAPTER FOURTEEN
EXPLORING ALTERNATIVE WORK SCHEDULES

The communications and computer revolution, combined with the emerging role of women in the workforce and the varied and dynamic nature of the nuclear family, requires supervisors that can ably direct employees requiring a flexible work schedule. The old formula of nine-to-five with two weeks off for vacation is rapidly giving way to a host of alternative work schedules designed to meet the individual needs of the employees while maintaining the same level of productivity and efficiency for the organization.

This chapter focuses on some of the more popular alternative work schedules or "flex-time" schedules as they are popularly called, examines other possible variations in work schedules, and will help you to answer these questions:

□ In what industries has flex-time already been implemented?
□ Which public and private agencies have undertaken studies in this field?
□ What are the various flex-time schedules that can be implemented?
□ Which schedules may fit the needs of your staff?

The Time Has Come

Flex-time is a working arrangement whose time has come. Here's a brief sampling of some industries and companies in which alternative work schedule programs have already been devised:

★ Life Insurance Industry—Connecticut Mutual Life, Travelers Insurance Company, Guardian Life Insurance Company of

America, Prudential Insurance Company of America, and Phoenix Mutual Life Insurance Company.
★ Oil Refiners and Distributors—Shell Oil Company and Exxon Corporation
★ Office Equipment Manufacturers—Hewlitt Packard Company, Pitney Bowes Inc., Xerox Corporation, and Honeywell.
★ Nondurable Goods Manufacturers—General Foods Corporation, Bristol Myers Company, Pfizer Inc., and Topps Chewing Gum.
★ Airlines—Lufthansa Airlines, American Airlines and many others.

Moreover, a growing body of literature exists which documents program benefits. Information from several public and private agencies that have contributed to the research and development of alternative work schedules is available from:

★ American Management Association
135 West 5 th St.
New York, NY 10020
★ McGraw-Hill and Company
1221 Avenue of the Americas
New York, NY 10020
★ The Ford Foundation
32 East 43rd St.
New York, NY 10017
★ McDonald's Corporation
McDonald's Plaza
Oak Brook, IL 60521
★ Communications Workers of America
1925 K St., NW
Washington, DC 20006
★ U.S. Senate Subcommittee on Labor
U.S. Senate Hart Bldg.
Washington, DC 20510
★ National Council for Alternative Work Patterns
46 S. Beach Road
S. Burlington, VT 05401

Eight Hours Flextime, With Core Time

Under this plan, employees may come to work at any time between, say, 7a.m. and 9:30 a.m. and depart eight hours later

100

taking into allowance corporate policy on time allocated for lunch. Core time refers to those hours in which employees must be on site or at the assigned work station. Often core time will be from 1 a.m. to 12 noon, from 1:30 to 3:30 p.m. or a long period such as 1 a.m. to 3 p.m. An established core time affords the supervisor the ability to schedule meetings with staff who may be otherwise arriving and departing from work at varying times.

Flexible Time	Core Time	Flexible Time

7:00 a.m.   9:00 a.m.   **CHART 14**   3:00 p.m.   5:00 p.m.

Variable Day

This plan is much like that above except the number of hours worked per day may vary as long as core time is maintained and the total hours per week add up to 40 (or the assigned amount). Some employers set a maximum of 10 hours per day.

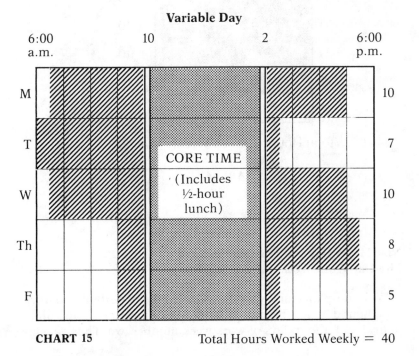

Variable Day

CHART 15   Total Hours Worked Weekly = 40

Four 10-Hour Days

A popular plan with employees is to be permitted to work four 10-hour days, four days a week with one week day off per week. This week day is usually fixed, which affords supervisors and managers ease and ability to schedule meetings, use equipment, and allocate other organizational resources.

One potential drawback to this plan is that many employees cannot effectively maintain productivity for the duration of the work day, thus the supervisor effectively gains only eight hours of productive output from the employee for the equivalence of four days while the organization paid them for the equivalence of five days. For those employees, however, that can maintain productivity, this plan can be mutually beneficial.

4-Day Week

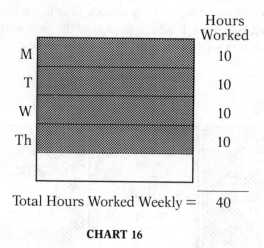

	Hours Worked
M	10
T	10
W	10
Th	10

Total Hours Worked Weekly = 40

CHART 16

Nine Hours Days, Alternating Four and Five Day Work Weeks or "5-4/9"

With this plan employees are afforded the opportunity to work nine-hour days for five days of work week number one, and nine-hour days for four days of work week number two. Thus, an employee on this plan will work a total of 81 hours over nine days. Usually the second Friday of the two-week period is the day that is taken off, although this may vary subject to individual working arrangement.

Good employees that tend to come in a little early and tend to leave a little late may like this plan as it rewards them with 26 more days off per year while only requiring a slightly longer day than they put in anyway. From the company's standpoint this is a sound plan because there's less likelihood of the fatigue or low productivity factor with the nine-hour day than with the ten-hour day.

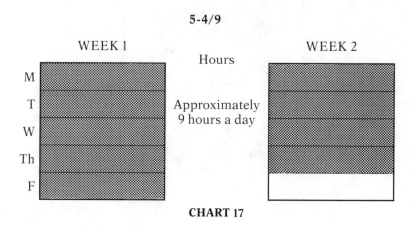

5-4/9

CHART 17

10-9-8-7-6

Under this plan employees put in long days at the beginning of the week often starting with ten hours on Monday, decreasing the number of hours by one Tuesday through Friday. This plan affords supervisor and employees the ability to get into high gear early in the week while being able to progressively leave earlier each day towards the week-end. This work schedule is advantageous for employees who are better workers at the beginning of the week or find it difficult to maintain the same pace by the fourth or fifth work day.

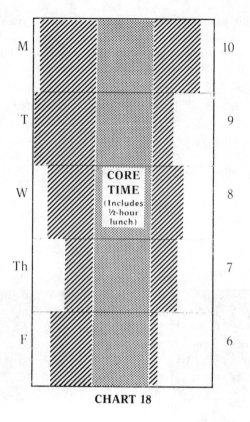

M		10
T		9
W	CORE TIME (Includes ½-hour lunch)	8
Th		7
F		6

CHART 18

On-Site, Off-Site

With the growing sophistication of remote terminals, personal computers and other on-line devices, an increasing number of employees can effectively execute tasks and responsibilities at home or from other off-site work places. Under this arrangement the supervisor stays in touch with the employee by telephone, electronic message or other device during those days the employee is off-site. On-site responsibilities, reporting, and meetings are scheduled to ensure that productivity and effectiveness are maintained; supervisor and employee can have first-hand contact and feedback with one another; and the employee gains the necessary social interaction and feeling of team or organizational spirit that may be vital for morale and organizational loyalty.

The Six-Day Work Week

Depending on your type of operation and the company's location the 6-day work week may be advantageous for some. Under this plan employees or staff come in to work six days per week generally for six hours and 40 minutes Monday through Saturday. Productivity studies have shown that this plan can be extremely effective because employees working under seven hours per day can maintain a high degree of productivity and efficiency. This plan is particularly useful for those pursuing advanced degrees or some other program of study, or for whatever reason prefer to depart early each day.

Looking ahead

In the years ahead changes in the work place may come at an even more accelerated pace. Modular office components, increasing use of temporary and subcontracted services, voice recognition technology and a host of emerging developments all but ensure that the work place of the last 80's may well experience a profound shift.

Already some data and word processing centers, research and development laboratories, maintenance and repair, and other organizational components are employed around the clock to optimize investment in plant and equipment or other organizational resources.

For a few employees, particularly those involved in physical activity for at least some portion of the work day, three-day work weeks of 13 hours and 2 minutes (every other day) may be possible. For others, work scheduling may consist of a creative approached based on a 16-hour or 168-hour work month.

Today's effective supervisor must be prepared to meet the challenge of what Alvin Toffler calls "third-wave society," wherein the very notion of the traditional work week, for many, may soon disappear. Moreover, companies and organizations that do not meet the varied needs of employees through flexible or alternative work schedules, may find their ability to compete for labor resources hampered.

Here's a quick run down on the flex-time programs discussed in this chapter:

☐ **Eight Hours Flex-time, With Core Time**—8 hour days, variable arrival and departure time while maintaining presence during core time.

- [ ] **Variable Day**—total hours worked equals 40, the employee has the option of varying the length of each work day while maintaining presence for a pre-established core time, and the maximum time per day that may be credited to the total work week is approximately 10 hours.
- [ ] **Four-Day Week**—most commonly involves four consecutive 10-hour workdays.
- [ ] **5-4/9**—employee works five consecutive days, approximately nine hours a day. During following work week, employee works four consecutive days, approximately nine hours a day. Pattern of week one and two is repeated thereafter.
- [ ] **10-9-8-7-6**—good for those who work best early in the week.
- [ ] **On-site, Off-site**—increasing occurrence with emergence of personal computer technology.
- [ ] **6 Day Work Week**—6 days of six hours and 4 minutes yields high productivity; useful for evening students.

Now, what factors lead and stimulate creativity and give an added dimension to your performance? Turn to Chapter 15.

CHAPTER FIFTEEN

NURTURING YOUR CREATIVITY

Eric Lowe supervised a staff of 8 in the credit and finance division of a large Dallas-based department store chain. He noticed that when the temperature in his office was a bit on the high side he wasn't able to think as clearly as he'd like to. Eric also felt quite certain that he did his best creative thinking very early in the morning before everyone else came in and that this was facilitated by a good cup of coffee or possibly a ginger ale or a diet cola. Often he walked over to and sat in the upholstered chair in his office but concluded that while it was comfortable he really didn't get much accomplished when sitting there.

If you've ever wondered what factors help to nurture your creativity, this is your chapter. In it look for the answers to the following questions:

- ☐ What **factors** lead to errors and unproductive activity?
- ☐ What kind of **weather** do most people report aids their creative thinking process?
- ☐ How can you determine what **time of day** is best for you to undertake a creative challenge?
- ☐ What are **other factors** that stimulate or hinder the creative thought process?

Control Your Environment

Many supervisors, just like Eric, start the day with a burst of energy hoping for a flash of inspiration and a little time to themselves to think. While it's not always possible to control your work environment just as you'd like to, there are many elements that should be addressed immediately. Poor lighting or poor ventilation would cramp anyone's style. World renowned speaker and management consultant Dave Yoho, president of Dave Yoho and Associates in Fairfax, Virginia, uses full spectrum lighting so that his employees will be more alert and energetic each day. Full spectrum lighting is available at most hardware and lighting stores.

Excessive noise, too little working room or extreme temperatures will hamper your creative capabilities.

What's the Weather?

Do you realize that most people do some of their best creative thinking when it is raining, snowing, overcast or storming? The reasons for this aren't exactly clear, but perhaps a nice day filled with bright sunshine is a foil to the creative thinking process. As we saw in chapter eight, good weather is a distraction, certainly, to many. While you can't schedule a rainy day in advance, it does make good sense to take advantage of what nature has to offer. If you're one of those people who does think creatively when the weather outside is frightful, why not "go with the flow." Look over that long-term plan that's been sitting in your upper drawer for the past several weeks. Or, schedule your staff for a brain-storming session (Chapter 19) to overcome current problems.

What Time Is It?

N.A.S.A. consultant Paul Blanchard, Ph.D., likes to rise at about 10 or 11 a.m. and retire at 2 a.m. to capture "the best times of the day." Most individuals find that their highest period of creativity is early in the morning while a significant number find that their peak period is midmorning or late at night. A far lesser number find their most creative time in the evening and less than one in 12 people judge himself to be creative during the afternoon.

If you're not sure what time of day you are at your creative best, monitor yourself over a one or two-week period. This can be done by keeping a time log of what activities you undertake and when, and also by noting your energy level and enthusiasm throughout the various parts of each day. (Note: also see Chapter Ten, "Supervising Cycles of Productivity.")

As a result of keeping this log you may be surprised to find that you should perhaps schedule meetings, write reports, or undertake professional reading on a different schedule than you've been doing.

Maybe These Help Creativity

Other factors that may be conducive to your personal creativity include, but are not limited to:

☐ wearing comfortable clothes
☐ having extra space on your immediate desk (a desk is not a filing cabinet!)
☐ using your favorite writing instrument
☐ changing your physical posture (i.e., walking, pacing, standing)
☐ readjusting the height of your seat
☐ altering the firmness or softness of your seat
☐ experimenting with the type, size and color of paper used to write on

To further stimulate your thinking, I suggest reading *A Whack on the Side of the Head* by Roger von Oech, Ph.D. (Warner Books). It is loaded with creative thought provoking strategies and methods.

These Could Hinder Creativity

While there's no hard evidence, it's quite possible that these factors could hinder your creative thought process and thus should at least be considered:

☐ the ring of your phone
☐ the color of your office walls
☐ the presence or absence of background sounds
☐ the feeling of impending interruptions
☐ the feeling that just sitting and thinking does not look productive
☐ too little sleep
☐ too much sleep
☐ heavy breads, pasta, or meats for lunch; also a high fat meal
☐ missing breakfast
☐ scheduling too tightly
☐ fear of criticism

Look around your office and the offices that surround you. Are there factors that you can identify that inhibit your creativity? If so, determine if you can effectively remove or diminish them.

Worth Fighting For

If you're like most managers or supervisors you've undoubtedly experienced days and weeks on end when you hardly had a moment to think, let alone a moment to undertake highly creative thinking. This is a serious mistake and one that should not continue to be given "back burner" status. As supervisor, your ability to effectively schedule yourself and your staff for greatest output depends upon your ability to nurture your creativity.

Here's a checklist of some of the key items presented in this chapter:

☐ Control your environment—eliminate poor lighting, poor ventilation, excessive noise, too little working room or extreme temperatures.
☐ Take advantage of rainy days.
☐ Determine your creative hours.
☐ Leave extra space on your desk.
☐ Use your favorite pen
☐ Get comfortable
☐ Eliminate factors that could hinder your creativity.

In section III which starts on page 111, we'll examine how to ensure that productivity can flourish through effective communication between you and your staff.

SECTION III

COMMUNICATING WITH STYLE

Effective communication between you and your staff is probably the single most important ingredient for both short and long-term success. This section examines the importance of emphasizing objectives to your staff—be they your organization's, your department's or your project team's. We'll also look at what you can do to foster a climate in which motivated employees can perform at their best and what steps you can take as supervisor to avoid demotivation." Chapter 18 offers advice on how to handle the data processing professional, a topic which can be of great importance to you if you have little experience in this area.

Other chapters in Section III focus on keeping a good thing going, working with the underachiever and excelling in communications. Chapter 20 offers a unique system for "improving the quality of interruptions" that you endure during the workday.

After completing Section III you should have a better understanding of how the timing, content, and quality of your communications affects the outlook and performance of both you and your staff.

CHAPTER SIXTEEN
EMPHASIZING OBJECTIVES

Every working day thousands of individuals are hired, and while each may have a fair and accurate description of the duties and responsibilities for which he/she was hired, the vast majority have no real information regarding organizational **goals** and **objectives**.

It is a mistake on the part of the supervisors to think that merely discussing an employee's role will provide sufficient information so that the employee may perform adequately and provide the organization, division or department with a fair return for the dollars invested (e.g., in salary, benefits, etc.).

Every employee should be required to read and retain a written statement of goals and objectives. Meetings should be held regularly to discuss how the individual departments or project teams facilitate the accomplishment of the company objectives.

This chapter discusses several reasons why it is vital that your staff understand your overall objectives, as well as those of the organization, and poses these questions:

☐ How can you get everyone working towards the same basic objective(s)?

☐ Can departments with seemingly competing interests work in unison?

☐ How does emphasizing project goals help demystify your behavior?

☐ What one question can employees ask themselves, in your absence, that will help guide their activities?

☐ Why should goals and objectives be quantified?

☐ Is a better directed and informed employee more productive?

All in Unison

One of the easiest ways to induce an entire organization to work toward the same basic objectives is to ensure that those **objectives are known** by each and every employee. When all employees understand the organization's objectives, there is greater potential for every working minute of every day to be better directed towards those objectives. The same holds true on a project or department level, and in communicating with your staff.

The pay-off in pursuit of organizational objectives can be dramatic. For example, 30 minute periods traditionally wasted at the start or conclusion of each day, might otherwise be used by employees to achieve that extra effort in contributing to overall objectives (also see Chapters 12 & 13).

Assembling the Team

Having all employees fully cognizant of organizational objectives increases the effectiveness of smaller teams at the division or department level. It's far easier for employees with seemingly competing interests to be part of the larger team when the accomplishment of objectives is everyone's chief priority. By adhering to the organizational objectives, some of the perceived "inherent" differences in viewpoint between divisions or departments will diminish.

For example, the sales division of the marketing department is keenly interested in increasing the level of sales activity in the next year. The quality control division within the production department, however, is keenly interested in producing only high quality products that pass inspection.

Based on the internal capacity of the company, the quality control division may feel that only a limited number of units of a certain product can be produced successfully. Lacking understanding of company objectives, the sales and quality control people in the above example could be forever at odds.

The sales staff and quality control staff can be united in their efforts, in light of the company's objectives. If one of the company's objectives for the coming year is to expand the sales base, achieve a defined level of growth, and penetrate new markets, then the quality control division may need to revise their standards downward somewhat, or arrange a meeting with the sales division to discuss the optimum level of output that the production department can achieve, in support of the sales division's compliance with company objectives.

Alternatively, if the company objective is to remain well entrenched in present markets, produce a high quality top-of-the-line product, and increase profitability on sales, then the sales division will have to adjust accordingly. This may include avoiding those customers for which sales fail to achieve a sufficient profitability level per unit sold (e.g., substantial delivery charges, difficult installation, or poor credit risks).

When I was in the MBA program at the University of Connecticut, Professor John Veiga had groups of us sit at a table and role play representing various seemingly competing divisions of the same company. Our goal was to reach policy decisions for the good of the company. We then viewed the process on video tape!

While conflicts between departments and divisions are predictable due to the nature and responsibility of the work performed, a team-like atmosphere can nevertheless be produced when all employees and all departments or divisions work toward the same ultimate objective(s).

Demystifies Mysterious Behavior

Informing your staff of objectives diminishes employees' perception of what appears to be mysterious behavior on your part. This is an overlooked, real benefit. Often, employees believe that the behavior of their supervisor is inconsistent.

114

You may be working in direct support of project objectives but employees that aren't aware of those objectives will not appreciate the job that you're doing.

Affords Unsupervised Employees Better Decision Making Ability

Since it is usually not possible to supervise every employee daily to the optimum degree, the next best step is to provide a set of guidelines or operating procedures from which your staff can make sound decisions. With a complete and clear picture of objectives, employees can make informed decisions in the absence of direct supervision.

In essence, unsupervised employees will be asking themselves "will this be good for the project/department/company/organization?" when they encounter a situation for which immediate supervisory feedback is not available.

Knowing the objectives will not provide every employee with clear-cut information as to how to proceed in every instance for which there is no supervision; however, in the long run, decision making capabilities will be improved.

The Need to Quantify

When informing staff of objectives, make sure that the objectives are **quantified** when possible. It is not enough to state as an objective, "We want to increase sales as much as possible." Instead say "We want to increase sales from108units to 132 units per year." Thus, each employee is afforded information as to the percentage or absolute number of the increase in unit sales to be achieved. Quantifying goals also enables employees to have a better understanding of how **their** contribution impacts the whole.

The communication and information that you receive from the bottom up, on the ease (or difficulty) in meeting quantified objectives, helps you in the role of supervisor. The feedback enables you to have a better understanding of what your tasks will be in achieving the quantified objective(s).

Not Fool-Proof

Informing your staff of objectives is by no means a fool-proof method for overcoming many of the ills that plague all organizations. However, a better **informed** and better **directed** employee will ultimately be a more **productive** employee. Even a minor increase in productivity at the individual level can have a ripple effect and contribute to a greater level of overall productivity and, hopefully, smoother and more profitable operations.

Here's a checklist on communicating objectives:

- ☐ Type, reduce, reprint and laminate goals and objectives for distribution to staff.
- ☐ Hold regular meetings which emphasize progress towards objective(s).
- ☐ De-mystify your behavior—let your staff know what you're doing.
- ☐ Avoid assuming that your staff comprehends its objective(s).
- ☐ Quantify goals and objectives.

Can you "motivate" your staff towards greater productivity? Since all motivation is really self motivation, Chapter 17 focuses on what you can do realistically to aid in the process.

CHAPTER SEVENTEEN
"MOTIVATING" YOUR STAFF

Keeping all employees "motivated" all the time is a near impossible task. Yet, as supervisor, you are often the driving force by which difficult tasks and activities can be accomplished by your staff. It's not enough to merely be a good scheduler or administrator; you must be a good "people" person.

Contemporary thought holds **that no one can motivate another; each individual must be motivated from within.** Yet we know that individuals will give an extra effort for a cause, for personal advancement for a leader.

What then, can be done to foster a climate conducive to generating that extra effort? In this chapter we'll canvass those management and supervisory techniques that enhance staff motivation and consider these questions:

☐ Does your enthusiasm encourage your staff?
☐ How often should praise be offered?
☐ How does delegation help in the motivation process?
☐ What is demotivation? Can the supervisor unknowingly cause this to occur?
☐ What are some characteristics of leadership?

Lead by Example

Studies by Likert, and Blake and Mouton and others support the notion that the participatory style of leadership is most effective in the long run. There are numerous ways to help achieve a climate conducive to a motivated staff. It is helpful to indicate your concern about your staff and maintain awareness of the individual problems and concerns of each. Encourage independent thinking, initiative, and resourcefulness. For your more competent staff members, work towards reducing the amount of supervision that they receive, thereby indicating your trust and reliance upon their capabilities.

If you are an enthusiastic type of supervisor and demonstrate this enthusiasm in your speech, mannerisms and behavior, this enthusiasm can be contagious to your staff and will help create a spirited atmosphere in which everyone is energized and raring to go. Remember, though, that a certain amount of pressure may be necessary with some to ensure that goals and objectives will be met. Only a small minority of workers are ever challenged to perform near their true capacity.

There are other ways to get the "motivation" ball rolling:

☐ **Offer praise** as often as possible and certainly where the employee undertakes a late afternoon, a new, or an especially difficult assignment. As Blanchard and Johnson appropriately say in the *One Minute Manager*, "Catch somebody doing something right."

☐ **Be receptive** to ideas from your staff. Learn from them and be open to all suggestions including those with little chance of working. This openness will enhance more creative thinking and more independent and happier employees.

☐ **Demonstrate your confidence** in your staff by what you say and what you do. Convey the belief that the tasks assigned can be performed effectively.

☐ **Focus on results** rather than methods for accomplishing tasks. This fosters creativity and ingenuity and keeps the team's approach to obstacles fresh and vibrant. I once supervised a person who approached tasks completely differently than I did, but uniformly achieved effective results!

☐ **Offer continuous feedback**. Let your staff members know how they're doing and where they stand.

☐ **Make the extra effort**. When you go out of your way to assist a staff member or incur some personal inconvenience, you are conveying a message that the success of your staff is your highest priority and that the real reason that you're a supervisor is to help them.

Raising Morale Through Delegation

The very nature of your tasks and responsibilities demands that some decision-making authority be turned over to your staff. The ability to delegate successfully will decrease your workload while increasing the productivity and morale of those you supervise.

Many supervisors, especially first-time supervisors, fear using delegation because they don't fully trust their staff or they've always been effective at taking care of everything themselves and can't break the habit of doing it all.

It's useful at this point to review the definition of supervisor. As we read in Chapter One, "a supervisor is one who tells people what to do and how to do it. A supervisor directly oversees the work of one or more individual employees while also maintaining many of his/her own operating duties—all in connection with the performance of a single cohesive function." Now, using this definition and acknowledging the principle of operating at the highest skill level, a supervisor's responsibility for delegation becomes clear.

Operating at the highest skill level essentially means that "no one should perform a task that can be performed just as well by someone who is paid less." Thus, the supervisor or manager who continues to "do it all" and avoids delegation when a staff member could in fact handle the task is supervising poorly and is likely to be incurring higher costs for his/her department or organization.

What, then, does the successful supervisor do to delegate effectively?

☐ Delegate to **employees who show enthusiasm**, initiative and interest and who have previously demonstrated the ability to handle and balance several tasks at once.

☐ Delegate enough **authority** for successful completion of the task by allowing key employees to make their own decisions, take initiative and continue operating even in your own absence.

☐ Delegate on a **piecemeal** basis—ensuring that employees are able to handle effectively what has been delegated to them and do not feel that they have been swamped or overloaded. Then as competence is demonstrated increase the complexity and frequency of the tasks to be delegated.

☐ **Prepare** your staff for delegation. This involves prior assessment of the employee's skills, interests and needs. You can even ask employees what new tasks and responsibilities they would like to assume.

☐ **Spend extra time** with those employees who are undertaking new challenges so that the delegation process proves effective.

Independent of your current level of delegation as supervisor, it's a good idea right now to examine all other tasks and responsibilities you currently maintain which could effectively be turned over to your staff.

Demotivation

While the management and psychological theorists maintain that we can only do so much to help "motivate" our staff and that motivation lies within, it is possible to demotivate staff through poor practices and behavior. Demotivation can mean any reduction in enthusiasm, initiative or output on the part of your staff as a result of something you've done.

Here are some ways that demotivation may occur:

★ **Scolding or belittling a staff member** particularly when others are around (See Chapter 22, Giving and Receiving Criticism)

★ **Being preoccupied** with your own activities and appearing selfish or manipulative of others

★ **Maintaining a favorite** among your staff that is obvious to everyone

★ **Being callous or insensitive** to employees' needs

★ Being **indecisive** when swift or forceful action or direction is called for

★ **Discussing shortcomings** of one employee with another

★ Using a staff member's employment to **coerce** him/her to perform a certain action

★ **Stifling employees' expression**, ideas and growth.

Many of the items cited above are elaborated more fully in Section IV, "Avoiding Supervisory Pitfalls," which begins on page 147 . Chapter 23, "How to Tell If You're a Bad Supervisor" in particular offers an in-depth look at demotivating behaviors and practices.

Supervisor as Leader

Professor Burt Scanlon of the University of Oklahoma has developed a leadership checklist that dovetails nicely with the supervisor's role as a motivational facilitator:

☐ Do I give employees adequate support?
☐ Do employees understand how to do the task assigned?
☐ Have I spelled out what's expected in terms of results?
☐ What have I done to cultivate a positive relationship?

- ☐ Does my staff have adequate freedom in which to work?
- ☐ What have I done to mentally and emotionally involve the staff in their jobs?
- ☐ Have employees been allowed to participate in setting goals and deciding means of achieving them?
- ☐ Have I shown adequate concern for employees as individuals?
- ☐ Have I shown adequate concern for employees' personal goals?
- ☐ Have I accurately assessed employees' strengths and weaknesses so that tasks are assigned which capitalize on strengths?
- ☐ Have I adequately and reasonably challenged my staff?

In the past several years the data processing professional has emerged. You may be assigned to supervise one or more data processing professionals. Chapter 18, "Handling the Data Processing Professional," explores ways to ensure that this employee becomes an active member of your team.

CHAPTER EIGHTEEN

HANDLING THE DATA PROCESSING PROFESSIONAL

Dick Lessar was hired by a Denver, Colorado based civil engineering firm to develop a project tracking system and improve the firm's use of computer graphics. Steve Pierson was Dick's supervisor. Steve had no real background in using data processing equipment and realized that he'd have to heavily rely on Dick in this area.

Dick was not like most of the other employees of the company. He seemed aloof and distant, and more interested in working on the terminal than interacting with others. Dick seemed to be marching to the beat of a different drum and sometimes appeared to be lost in space just staring at the screen.

While Steve had had substantial experience in effectively supervising others, Dick Lessar posed a new problem. Steve had no idea regarding how long specific computer-related tasks should take and thus how to best monitor Dick's activities.

What steps can a supervisor assigned to handle a data processing professional take to ensure that a team-like atmosphere and normal supervisory functions are maintained? This chapter provides such information and considers the following questions:

- [ ] How can a supervisor who's otherwise unfamiliar with data processing equipment **effectively supervise** a data processing professional?
- [ ] What should one **look for** in an effective data processing professional?
- [ ] What specific steps must be taken to ensure that the data processing professional is an **active part of** your project **team**?
- [ ] How can you **spot an ineffective** programmer?

A Staff Member is a Staff Member

Steve resolved that in working with Dick he would supervise in the same way that he did with his other staff members. Thus, Dick was responsible for attending all staff meetings and participating in staff meetings just like everyone else. This helped to prevent Dick from becoming isolated from the rest of the project team or developing the notion that the machinery that he worked with was more important than his peers or his company.

Reporting and Monitoring

Steve recalled the case of an earlier employee having data processing responsibilities who maintained a closed, almost secretive approach to handling tasks. Steve knew that loyalty comes from being part of a team and that a non-communicative employee or one that maintained privileged information, i.e., a corner on the market, was not healthy for the employee, the team or the company. Thus, Steve prepared specific goals and objectives in consultation with Dick, drew up a task list and timetable and met with Dick on a daily basis to review problems encountered and overall progress.

To increase Dick's understanding of the company's ongoing projects, Steve familiarized Dick with the current forms and controls in use and illustrated how information was handled and compiled. He also took Dick out to the field so that Dick could view first hand what was being accomplished and how his job supported company operations.

Assessing Dick's Work

Steve realized that no matter how much he learned about using data processing equipment, programming and computer graphics it would take him a long time to be able to evaluate the effectiveness of Dicks efforts. So Steve set up procedures whereby he could quickly gain the information he needed regarding Dick's performance.

First, Steve requested that all programs developed be accompanied by documentation, i.e., an English narrative, full code printing that explained the importance of each program element. Steve also established a peer coding review system whereby Dick's programs were examined by others having familiarity in this area.

Steve was then able to determine if Dick was developing forty lines of code when most other data processing professionals could accomplish the same task in say, twenty lines.

Profile of an Effective DP Professional

Steve read a little about managing in the computer age, talked with others and was able to produce a profile of an effective data processing professional:

- Frequently **asks** "when do you need to have it by?"
- Consistently **meets goals**.
- **Relies** on systems manuals—no one on planet Earth can memorize every nuance of every instruction of software and other data processing systems support materials. Successful professionals **use** the manuals.
- **Employs** standardized modular/component programs when available—in plain English, this means no reinventing of the wheel and no customized program development when adequate programs already exist.
- **Relies** on programming dictionaries.
- Is **sharp and articulate** just like other good employees. This also means avoiding using computer gobbledygook in explaining what's being done or what has to be done.

Detecting the Poor Data Processing Professional

Unfortunately, some data processing professionals cloak their ineffectiveness by inaccurately or inappropriately conveying "hardware" shortcomings. In reality the shortcomings are, more often than not, in their own capabilities. The poor professional may be using techniques and procedures learned three to five years ago while machine capability, software and support systems have increased exponentially.

The employee who says "I can't do this" or "This can't be done" may really be saying, "I don't know how to do this," or "My background is insufficient to accomplish what you've asked," or "The equipment may be fully capable of handling the task but I'm not sure on how to get started."

The data processing professional who says "Response time will suffer" is often offering a lame excuse. The more appropriate statement may well have been, "This will require three to five second search delays." Hardly worth canning a necessary function.

One final clue to the poor professional is the continued missing of self-determined target dates. For example, in consultation with the supervisor, if the employee says that goal XYZ can be accomplished in six working days, you offer eight days, and it's still not done by the tenth day, very few excuses will justify this prolonged execution time.

There's no magic and there's no mystery to working with data processing equipment. The time required to accomplish tasks requiring high doses of creativity and innovation, can be estimated much like non-DP tasks are.

In short, the notion that the data processing professional must be supervised differently than others is highly erroneous.

A good perspective by which to view the data processing function is that data processing equipment, software and systems support materials serve the business of your organization and ultimately, human needs.

Here's a checklist for effectively supervising the data processing professional:

- ☐ Treat the DP professional just like you treat any other staff member.
- ☐ Require that the DP professional report regularly.
- ☐ Familiarize him/her with the company's on-going project.
- ☐ Assess his/her work (get help if you have to).
- ☐ Require that programs developed be accompanied by documentation.
- ☐ Observe his/her use of systems manuals and standardized modular/component programs.
- ☐ Recognize that statements such as, "This can't be done" may be a cover for incompetence.
- ☐ Remember there are both good and bad DP professionals, and the good ones stand out just like other good employees stand out.

CHAPTER NINETEEN

INSTILLING A TEAM-LIKE
ATMOSPHERE

Michael Johnstone supervised a staff of six for a Tacoma, Washington real estate development corporation. Time and time again Michael would toss about the problems faced by his staff, work through solutions on his own and then call a meeting to announce what would be done. Frequently Michael's solutions were right on target, clearly addressed the problems at hand and could be effectively implemented with existing resources.

One might say that Michael was very effective in supervising and coordinating the activities of his staff. Yet, slowly he was "losing them." Michael's problem—**he was not involving his staff in the decision-making process**. Though the staff clearly recognized Michael's ability to create viable solutions to existing problems, each staff member felt somewhat disenfranchised from the "team" because he/she was not really able to participate or contribute to the creative problem solving process.

What steps can Michael take to continue to supervise as he sees fit while giving staff members a greater feeling of responsibility and instilling a more team-like atmosphere? In this chapter we'll explore the answers to the following:

- ☐ Why are decisions made by the team often more effective than those made by an individual?
- ☐ What **immediate benefits** are provided through group decision making or brainstorming?
- ☐ Why does the supervisor essentially **still get his/her way** even after posing problems to the group at large?
- ☐ What should be **encouraged** during brainstorming sessions?
- ☐ What are some of the **pitfalls** of group decision-making?

126

Deal 'em In

During the next few months a few of the staff members independently met with Michael to discuss the need to be more involved in decisions which affected their assigned tasks and workload. Michael had been reading about the dynamics of group decision-making in a highly respected supervisory management newsletter to which he subscribed.

Having confidence in his own abilities to effectively lead the group while allowing for more staff input, Michael prepared an agenda to be distributed to the staff in advance of their next meeting.

On this meeting agenda, Michael listed many of the traditional items that appeared on previous meeting agendas but this time also added a section entitled "Issues to be Resolved." He then went on to list several items all posed in the form of questions, under this heading.

In the few days before the meeting, Michael noticed that his staff was buzzing a bit more than usual and there seemed to be a more highly charged atmosphere within the office.

Surprise, Surprise

When meeting time came, Michael was ready as usual. However, what he didn't anticipate was that his staff was also ready—in top form. The meeting was rather routine as Michael passed over the early agenda items.

When it was time to discuss "Issues to be Resolved," the meeting came alive. Mary Witherspoon, who had barely said anything in the last meeting, had a list of alternatives prepared for many of the questions posed. Keith Groberg offered many suggestions. The other staff members each made a few good points during the balance of the meeting.

Michael was truly amazed. He had hoped that his new approach would encourage greater participation and achieve that more team-like atmosphere he was seeking. He was surprised that this had worked so well and so quickly.

Relying On The Team

What are the benefits a supervisor can enjoy when relying on the team to creatively approach problems and resolve issues?

1. **Group performance** is increased—**more participation** leads to more creative thinking which often leads to more feasible alternatives.
2. Poor or unworkable alternatives are more likely to be spotted—in group discussion with several minds working on the same problem the probability of someone **detecting an unworkable solution** is greatly increased.
3. **New issues are identified**—invariably discussion on how to resolve current issues facilitates the group's ability to identify other issues of potential importance. This aids the planning process, since these issues are often identified sooner by the group than if left to be discovered solely by the supervisor.
4. **More enthusiasm is generated**—individual staff members gain an added measure of enthusiasm when approaching tasks assigned to them when they know that the group is aware of and involved with what needs to be done.
5. **Objectives are reemphasized**—tying in with the information presented in Chapter 16 , group decision-making allows everyone to examine the issues to be resolved in light of the group's overall objectives.

Some managers and supervisors fear that allowing the staff to participate in the problem-solving process will diminish or subvert the supervisor's plans and ideas on how to successfully accomplish the project at hand. This is simply not true. As supervisor you still moderate the meeting, maintain strong influence regarding ideas and opinions expressed and lead the discussions as you see fit. Rather than subvert or thwart your role, getting your team involved enhances your position.

AND, OF COURSE, YOU ALL KNOW I STRESS INDIVIDUALITY & CREATIVITY....

Removing the Popcorn Popper Lid

One of the easiest ways to generate a high level of group participation is through brainstorming. To use brainstorming effectively, pose a question or problem to the group and then with magic marker or chalk in hand go up to the board and begin writing everything that comes out of the group. This is no time for qualifying any of the suggestions or recommendations offered. Simply record the ideas expressed as fast as they come and when the group feels that they have "wrung themselves out," stop.

Now, still encouraging group participation, go back to the list of ideas presented and stratify them into three groups. One group should consist of those ideas that can be quickly eliminated because of budget constraints, resource constraints or because they are obviously impractical or unworkable. Another group should consist of those ideas that appear to be gems. You may only get a few gems but that's all you usually need. The final group can consist of those ideas presented which the group feels may have some merit but are second tier to the gems.

Prepare three new lists, one for the gems, one for the second tier group and one for the eliminated group. Now, go back to the gems and discuss each one in more detail. The final solution for the issue being discussed may be formulated as a result of this group-wide discussion, or you may have to work on this a bit more on your own. Either way, you have effectively accelerated the process of resolving issues while instilling a team-like atmosphere.

In a similar manner, brainstorming can be used to handle the other issues that confront you. When soliciting the group during a brainstorming session, remember, **no idea is too outrageous.** Write them all down no matter how they sound at first hearing.

Often brainstorming sessions get a bit humorous as the collective creative energies of your staff foster a highly spirited, almost electric-type, atmosphere and many endorphins (positive nerve impulses) are fired. Also, one decision or alternative that can always be made when confronted by an issue, is to do nothing. Undoubtedly someone will offer that suggestion and it too should be recorded.

Pitfalls of the Group Process

There are a few things to look out for when involving your staff in the problem solving process. First, don't get lazy. More than one supervisor has gotten into the habit of letting the group provide all of the real creative thinking, and then over-rely on these sessions. Another factor to consider is the strong influence of a senior, dominant, or influential group member (other than yourself) whose thoughts and ideas are reflected more often and more strongly than others on your staff.

A third pitfall occurs when the group becomes more interested in arriving at a harmonious decision rather than focusing on an innovative, perhaps controversial, perhaps untested, but highly promising approach.

It's your job to keep these sessions balanced and on target, to use the ideas and suggestions generated when appropriate but to continue to maintain control and provide necessary direction.

Here's a review of some of the key points made in this chapter:

☐ **Distribute** an advance copy of your next meeting agenda to your staff.

☐ **Include** an "Issues to be Resolved" section.

☐ Remember that **team approaches** to creative problem solving are often far more effective than an individual approach.

☐ Use **brainstorming** to encourage even more ideas.

☐ **Avoid the pitfalls** of the group process—letting the group do all the real thinking, letting a senior member dominate, or allowing the group to strive for harmony rather than effective solutions.

☐ Keep creative problem solving sessions **balanced** and on target.

CHAPTER TWENTY

IMPROVING THE QUALITY
OF INTERRUPTIONS

Vic Morrel was the project manager of a staff of seven for a small consulting firm in the suburbs of Cincinnati. As project manager, Vic's main responsibility was to supervise his staff and ensure that all project deliverables were submitted on time. Vic was an effective delegator and had taken considerable time and effort to map out a workable project plan which fully involved all of his staff.

On a daily basis, however, Vic was taking a professional beating. Each of his staff members averaged about three to five visits to his office each day for a variety of questions and issues regarding project activities. Though Vic took the time to schedule well run, informative meetings and individually met with staff members in their offices, he couldn't seem to stem the tide of interruptions that were virtually burning him out by the end of each day.

What options does a supervisor have for reducing the number of staff-related interruptions per day and improving the quality of interruptions that do have to be made?

This chapter spotlights a simple system for "improving the quality of interruptions" while maintaining overall effectiveness with your staff, and offers answers to the following questions:

- [ ] Why is the establishment of a priority system for interruptions essential?
- [ ] How does such a system provide employees with a framework for taking action?
- [ ] How does such a system promote greater staff interaction?
- [ ] What is the greatest payoff to you in initiating a priority system for interruptions?
- [ ] What is the greatest payoff for the entire staff by initiating such a system?

The Ten Thousandth Interruption

Returning to Vic's situation, the number of interruptions per day seemed to be increasing. Slowly, Vic realized that his effectiveness was diminishing. He was becoming cross and irritable with his staff and couldn't wait for the end of the day to unwind. In the evening, at home, he would toss around ideas for reducing the number of interruptions but none of them seemed to be the answer. He had thought of closing his door for several hours each day or on particular days but was afraid that someone might be let down at a crucial moment. He considered elaborate scheduling, message and memo systems, and other exotic methods but quickly determined that they would involve a great deal of effort with, perhaps, no real improvement in operations.

A week or two passed and Vic acknowledged that he would have to come up with a solution for the sake of his staff and for the sake of his own health. He decided to keep a log of staff related interruptions over a three-day period. At the end of three days, after carefully reviewing the log, he had the answer. Many of the questions for which his staff was interrupting him could be answered by carefully reviewing the project plan. Other staff questions could be answered by co-workers, and still other questions required a yes or no or short answer that only necessitated using the inter-office intercom.

After this careful examination of the nature of the questions asked and the resulting interruptions, Vic was ready to install his plan.

The V-4 System

Vic assembled his staff and announced that a new and innovative way for handling questions and project-related problems was going to be introduced. Vic called this the "V-4 System." Here's how it works:

V-1 Questions—A V-1 question consisted of any question or concern that could be answered simply by referring to the project plan, orientation kit or project meeting notes which had already been circulated to all staff members.

Easily 25% of the questions being brought to Vic could be answered by employees on their own by consulting these readily available project materials. Upon hearing this the staff members acknowledged that now and then they had been a little lazy and were using Vic in a manner that was perhaps somewhat inappropriate.

V-2 Questions—The V-2 question consists of anything a staff member may ask which can effectively be answered by another staff member, once again reducing the number of interruptions that Vic must endure.

One might readily observe that the V-2 question doesn't reduce the number of overall interruptions that the staff must endure, it merely shifts some interruptions on Vic to others. This is true. However, any distribution of interruptions among and between the staff would be more equitable on a personal basis than having the supervisor bear the brunt. Upon hearing this, the staff immediately agreed that it was more equitable to resolve V-2 type questions by using other staff members.

V-3 Questions—A V-3 Question consists of those concerns of employees that must be presented to Vic and for which it would be inappropriate to ask another. The V-3 question, however, could be answered by a yes or a no or in one or two sentences. Thus, the need for a staff member to walk over to Vic's office and seek face-to-face communication was unnecessary.

V-3 questions are easily handled by the office intercom which is still an interruption, but of far less magnitude than an office visit. Once again the staff agreed that they had been derelict in the use of the inter-office intercom and here-after would more frequently engage in this simple technology.

V-4 Questions—The V-4 question is that, which having exhausted V-1, V-2, and V-3 options, can only be resolved by a close encounter of the fourth kind—meeting with Vic in person and spending some time working out the best way as to how to proceed.

Vic explained to his staff that he had no problem whatsoever being interrupted for V-4 type questions. In fact, he encouraged his staff to consult him personally any time that a V-4 question was encountered. The key here is that after exploring V-1, V-2 and V-3 options, less than 2% of all questions fall into the V-4 category. Thus, Vic was effectively able to reduce the number of interruptions per day from 20-35, to 3-8!

Benefits of the V-4 System

Let's step back now and examine the benefits of the V-4 system. First, it provides the staff with a framework for taking action. In accordance with the recommendations made in chapter 15. "Emphasizing Objectives," the V-4 system enables your staff to continue making progress even in your absence.

It also helps to promote greater staff interaction and more sharply defines your role to the staff. When you are no longer observed as the "den mother" that handles every little question and concern, you provide your staff with the opportunity to more fully appreciate your proper role as supervisor and the importance of your time.

The greatest benefit to you is that your time is effectively increased while not markedly diminishing anyone else's time. With less small interruptions, your creative thinking and planning time has been increased.

Later, Vic enrolled in an evening course on stress management so that he could understand better how to keep himself in top form. "By acknowledging and strengthening one's glandular vulnerabilities," says the Creative Wellness Lady—Michelle Lusson, renown author of *Creative Wellness*, "one can effectively achieve personal stress, health and image management."

For a handy review, here's a checklist for the V-4 system (this time in descending order):

- □ V-4—for those questions and concerns that you must **answer in person**.
- □ V-3 —those items that can be handled via the office **intercom**.
- □ V-2—those items that can be **handled by co-workers**.
- □ V-1—those questions and concerns that are addressed and readily available in **project related materials**.
- □ **Enroll** in a course on, or **read** about, stress management.

Chapter 21 investigates the successful supervisor's role and communication in "Working With the Underachiever."

CHAPTER TWENTY-ONE

WORKING WITH THE UNDERACHIEVER

Ted Knowles was supervisor in a large division of a major insurance company in Chicago. Most of the employees that Ted supervised were well-adjusted, veteran employees of the company with whom Ted had a fine working relationship. There was one employee, however, Ted found hard to understand. Dennis Sanders was unhappy most of the time, maintained what Ted felt was a poor professional attitude, and, on occasion, had a lower level of performance than many of his co-workers.

Ted strongly felt that it was within Dennis' potential to become a good employee and a satisfactory performer. In addition, Ted resolved that, as supervisor, it was his responsibility to get to the root of Dennis' problems, for the good of Dennis, the company, and himself.

This chapter is a case history of events that actually occurred and the checklist below will be the only one presented. (The names used in the case history have been changed.)

Let's discover now what steps Ted took to improve the situation, including:

- ☐ identifying short and long term goals
- ☐ establishing formal authority
- ☐ assigning new responsibilities
- ☐ instilling confidence
- ☐ maintaining an environment of mutual respect, and providing career advancing opportunities.

Investigate First

Over the next several weeks Ted made extensive efforts to subtly investigate possible causes for Dennis' behavior. Ted learned that Dennis felt unchallenged in his current position which he had occupied for over four years. Dennis also had a desire for more independence and increased responsibility; something that previous supervisors had failed to acknowledge.

While Ted was not exactly new—he had been with the organization for two years—he also learned that Dennis tended to resent new symbols of authority—anyone who has been with the company for fewer years than Dennis.

As if these problems weren't enough, Ted also discovered that Dennis had a pronounced lack of self confidence and self esteem and fostered the notion that management and co-workers had low confidence in him. Combined with Dennis' self-admitted poor communication ability, the portrait of a very unhappy and unproductive employee emerged.

Turning the Tide

The story of Dennis Sanders is not so unusual; surveys point to widespread worker discontent and maladjustment in contemporary business (see Section I, Introduction). The challenge facing Ted is not uncommon either though many supervisors never accept the challenge of helping a losing employee to adopt winning ways.

Let's examine a variety of methods for achieving optimal performance by a heretofore underachiever.

Identify Short and Long Term Goals

The employee needs to clearly identify specific short and long term goals for himself or herself and work with management on what needs to be done to achieve these goals. It is possible that the employee has no goals or only vague goals or has lost sight of any goals that were originally established. This situation is like having a ship without a rudder that ultimately founders. It is the supervisor's responsibility to sit down with the employee and formally set goals in writing and plan steps to reach those goals in detail.

Establishing Formal Authority

Ted's authority as supervisor had never formally been established in Dennis' mind. In large part this is often due to the fact that neither the previous supervisor, or top management had ever issued a written directive defining the formal working relationship. As simple as this procedure may seem, it is often necessary before some employees can ultimately accept a change in supervisors.

In addition, many employees need to comprehend their place in the formal structure of the organization or, specifically, the division and to see where they stand in relation to new staff. A sense of insecurity can arise from having an uncertain status and the unhappy employee has a special need to be informed.

New and Appropriate Responsibilities

Dennis wants more responsibility and more independence, yet suffers from poor communication ability and interpersonal skills. This suggests that he is task-oriented as opposed to people-oriented. The supervisor should present as many different challenging tasks as the employee can handle in this situation

The question arises, however: are these tasks available in Dennis' current position? As changes occur within the division and throughout the organization, an employee who remains relatively stationary must be afforded new and challenging tasks lest he feel that the world is passing him by.

Instill Confidence

The supervisor must praise the insecure employee more often and more clearly. The employee should always know when he or she has done a good job and be given feedback as soon as possible. A couple of compliments a day from the supervisor can keep the doctor away.

It should also be made clear to the employee in a private session or staff meeting that the supervisor does have confidence in the employee and expects the employee to maintain the good performance standard and good attitude of which he/she is capable.

Defuse the Time-Bomb

It would be over simplistic to suggest that Dennis' personal and professional problems will simply float away through proper supervision. There are steps that can be taken, however, to diffuse an employee's confrontational, abrasive mannerisms. The supervisor, leading by example, should turn the other cheek, ignore unwarranted remarks, and strive to maintain an environment of mutual respect. Hostility must be met with patience and fairness along with the aforementioned praise whenever possible.

Large doses of patience and understanding do not, however, mean that discipline standards be dropped. If an employee arrives late, spends excessive time on the phone, takes long lunches, and engages in otherwise unproductive practices, the correction of these deficient habits is a step towards improvement in other areas.

Onward and Upward

It's also important that the employee be informed as to the quickest road for advancement and more responsibility. The employee must be informed that by increasing his or her level and range of skills he or she increases potential for career advancement and earnings.

Employees that keep doing the same job well year after year usually end up feeling like they're in a rut. The employee must be encouraged to get cracking—open up those training books, attend those courses and **volunteer** to take on new or extra assignments.

Clean Up Your Own Backyard

The supervisor must continue to approach the goals and objectives of the division with enthusiasm, all the while displaying eagerness in working with the unproductive, unhappy employee. The supervisor who maintains negative thoughts about interacting with this employee will not be able to disguise these thoughts effectively and this will put a damper on the relationship. The employee will sense it and respond negatively.

Converting a losing employee to a winner requires nothing less than the erasure of all negative thoughts the supervisor may hold, replacing them with a positive attitude and visible enthusiasm towards the employee. In short, the supervisor leads the employee instead of the other way around.

Saving an employee on a sinking ship is no easy task. Moreover, no management system or school of thought has yet devised a fool-proof method for dealing with unhappy, low-performance employees.

CHAPTER TWENTY-TWO
GIVING AND RECEIVING CRITICISM

Ruth Decker supervised a staff of eight in the office of personnel of the county government. Robert Hodges was the youngest and most recent addition to Ruth's staff. One week, Ruth had to attend a management training program in the western part of the state and needed Robert to finish a report for the county manager by the time she returned at the end of the week. Over the telephone, Ruth very carefully outlined for Robert what needed to be done and how she could be reached if he ran into problems.

Two days later, on Wednesday, Ruth had not received a call from Robert and thus assumed that he was encountering little difficulty in undertaking the assignment. On mid-afternoon of Thursday Ruth returned and was pleased to see Robert's typed, finished report on her desk ready for review and hopefully, ready for submission on Friday.

After just a few minutes Ruth realized that Robert had missed the mark on some of the points made on the report, had completely left out one small section and had prepared a poor conclusion. Given that the report was to be delivered the following day, Ruth was rather upset.

Her immediate reaction was to take the report over to Robert's office and in strong language ask why he hadn't sought help and why the report had various shortcomings. Report in hand she marched in the direction of Robert's office and stopped a few paces from the door. Robert was discussing a new task with another of Ruth's staff people. Ruth looked at her watch and noticed it was about 3:30 and headed back to her own office.

Coolly and calmly thinking through the situation she decided that the report was indeed salvageable and that in an undisturbed 45 to 60 minutes she could probably shore up its weak points. resubmit it to the production staff and still have it available Friday morning.

About an hour later she was finished and the report was ready to be retyped. She made an extra copy which reflected the changes that she added so that her subsequent discussion with Robert would involve mild criticism mixed with supervisory assistance. In this chapter we'll review both giving and receiving criticism and provide answers to the following:

- ☐ What is the best time of the day and week to criticize employees?
- ☐ When should you never criticize?
- ☐ Where should the criticism be offered?
- ☐ What are some effective ways to handle criticism levied at you?
- ☐ How can you handle the chronic complainer?

Criticizing Without Crushing

Ruth finally got together with Robert on Friday morning and reviewed his report paragraph by paragraph. Ruth pointed out the strong points and the weak points and left Robert with a copy. She then emphasized that although it was not desirable to issue the assignment by a long distance telephone and to follow up using the same, it's what the situation called for. She explained to Robert that by calling for assistance while the report is in progress everyone saves time.

Robert agreed that what she said made sense and that he would follow her directions more closely in the future. By handling the situation in this manner Ruth was able to provide constructive criticism to Robert that both conveyed her present concerns, offered assistance and established a solid working relationship for the future.

Let 'em Have It Early

Numerous management analysts agree that the best time to dispense employee criticism is early in the day and early in the week. This affords the opportunity to speak to the employee again some time during the day in a more casual, lighthearted way to assure the employee that everything is all right, that you criticized the performance or behavior, but not the person, and that you have confidence in the employee's ability to continue to handle or assume responsibilities.

Criticizing late in the day poses several problems. First you may end up sending an employee home who's worried or anxious about his/her job—unnecessarily so. Also, you and your staff are often tired at the end of the day and any criticism or strongly worded message can be taken out of context or overblown because of the fatigue.

The same holds true for the employee whom you criticized just before a week-end, vacation or holiday.

Cool Down

There's an old Chinese proverb which says, "Never write a letter when you're angry." An analogy when dispensing criticism could be "Never criticize when you're angry." Use whatever delaying process you can to put time between when you initially feel the need to criticize an employee and when you actually do it. You'll be more objective, your criticism will be more constructive and your overall employee communications will be vastly improved.

Conversely, don't wait too long to dispense the criticism after the poor performance has been identified. As with justice, criticism is best dispensed quickly.

Criticize In Private

The reason why Ruth stopped on her way into Robert's office was that someone else was in Robert's office. Ruth instinctively knew that it was inappropriate to criticize Robert in front of another staff member and not to enable him to have the benefit of a quiet, extensive, closed-door session in which his viewpoint could be aired. Ruth also knew that discussing one employee's shortcomings with another was a disguised, malevolent form of criticism. Conversely, she was quick to praise, particularly in the earshot of others and thus was perceived as a supervisor who communicated with style.

Receiving Criticism

You're not the only one who feels the need to criticize. On occasion, your staff does too. Their criticism is often muted, concealed or disguised in the form of a suggestion. Whether you call these criticisms, complaints, grievances or suggestions, author Ray A. Killian offers a four point system for receiving criticism.

1. **Be courteous**—Treating an employee courteously while he/she is offering feedback greatly affects his/her attitude. One way to convey your concern is to **take notes** of what is being said and then repeat the essential elements so the employee is assured that you have full comprehension. You may even wish to **thank the employee** for bringing this item to your attention and let him/her know that you'll give it fair consideration.

2. **Gather information**—Review the complaining employee record, if just to determine that the employee is not a "chronic complainer." Is he/she absent, non-productive, uncooperative or a poor performer? Realistically, this will color your perception of and reaction to the problem addressed.

3. **Take appropriate action**—If the criticism or suggestion is justified, tell the employee what you intend to do to improve the situation. If the complaint is unjustified "be firm and calm in telling the employee so." Another possibility exists. The suggestion or criticism made could be focused on something that cannot be changed. This may take some doing, but attempt to explain why this is so.

WHY BILL ... HOW CONSIDERATE OF YOU TO CHECK THE LEVEL OF THIS DESK ....

ZZZ...!!

4. Follow-up—When the employee's grievance or suggestion was valid and helped you to better execute your responsibilities or helped the department or organization in some way, let him or her know in at least a week or two. Often that which is suggested by employees can improve overall efficiency.

James O. MacDonald, in *Management Without Tears*, offers some suggestions on handling chronic complainers. MacDonald advocates a put up or shut up approach. This involves asking the complainer to "prepare a written analysis of the problems and to propose solutions." If the complainer doesn't follow through you can then convey the message that next time "a written analysis will again be requested." If the complainer does submit a written analysis it can then be evaluated on its own mertis. MacDonald sees this as a no-lose situation.

The hallmark of a successful supervisor is being able to give and receive criticism effectively. It has been said that "You're as big as what irritates you." If you let the small grievances and complaints of your staff get to you, and every staff has them, then you'll overreact and needlessly spend energy on brush fires, while missing forest fires.

If you establish a supportive, cooperative framework in which criticism can be both dispensed and received then you'll be perceived as an effective communicator and a highly effective supervisor.

Here's a review of the key points made in this chapter:

☐ **Criticize early** in the day and early in the week.
☐ **Avoid Criticizing** when you're angry.
☐ **Listen** to what the employee has to say.
☐ **Dispense** the criticism as **swiftly** as possible.
☐ **Criticize in private** and let the employee have a chance to explain.
☐ **Be courteous** when handling employee complaints.
☐ **Take notes** as to what's being said and then repeat essential elements to assure full comprehension.
☐ **Gather information** to determine if the employee is a chronic complainer.
☐ **Take appropriate action**, i.e., change and explain, explain if the complaint is unjustified, or explain if nothing can be done and why.

☐ **Follow-up** on the employee complaint a few weeks later by thanking them if operations have been improved.

☐ Handle the chronic complainer with a **put up or shut up** approach.

☐ **Establish an environment** in which both giving and receiving criticism can occur without being disruptive.

This concludes Section III, Communicating With Style. In Section IV, Avoiding Supervisory Pitfalls, seven chapters are presented to help guide you past potential problems that may occur as a result of your management style.

SECTION IV

AVOIDING SUPERVISORY PITFALLS

Supervisory pitfalls are easy to fall into. Since the perfect manager has never existed, at least some of what you do and how you do it is going to generate problems with, and for your staff. Chapters 23 through 29, which comprise Section IV, cover a wide area of supervisory pitfalls. Chapter 23, for example, "Determining If You're a Bad Boss," offers nine ways to examine if the way you supervise is making it difficult for others and if you're being perceived as a bad boss.

Chapter 29, "Playing Would-Be Lou Grant," examines the problem of the supervisor who regards himself/herself as "tough, but fair" but in reality is only tough.

The other chapters, such as "Failing to Listen," "Supervising Out of the Office," and "Undermining the Ideal Employee" offer unique and in-depth insights into the problems that may occur in the demanding and challenging role of supervisor. As in the previous sections and chapters presented in this book, a host of checklists and guidelines are provided that will enable you to quickly take the steps necessary to avoid, or get out of a supervisory pitfall.

CHAPTER TWENTY-THREE

HOW TO TELL IF YOU'RE A BAD SUPERVISOR

There are hundreds of books and articles available that tell us how to supervise or manage better, and how to get the most out of employees. This chapter focuses on how to tell if you're a bad boss—what behaviors, procedures and style you may be propagating inadvertently that may be demotivating staff, reducing overall productivity, or otherwise causing employees to regard you as a "bad boss."

Topics presented will include the practice of **maintaining fairness and consistency**, exploiting your staff, offering the continuing promise or the dangling carrot, and making light use of heavy terms among others.

This chapter will help you to come to grips with some poor practices that may be dividing you and your staff. Questions to be answered include:

- ☐ Why does **mistreating** one employee make you lose out with all the rest?
- ☐ Why is **no promise** better than a continuing one?
- ☐ When should **terms** such as "teamwork," "dedication" and "commitment" be used?
- ☐ What phrase indicates that you're **throwing curves to your staff?**
- ☐ Is **flexibility** important, and if so why?
- ☐ What **3 elements** must be balanced for the supervisor to be effective?

Unfair to One, Resented by All

If you strive to maintain consistency and fairness with all of your staff members except one or a few within your organization or department, you can quickly lose the respect of all. Strive to be consistent and fair with 100% of your staff. Most employees have a built-in sense of what is right and strongly dislike the ill treatments you may bestow upon a co-worker (independent of the specifics of the situation).

You would be better off as a supervisor, literally, to be unfair or inconsistent with all employees occasionally than with a select few regularly. Carefully review your employee roster now and assess whether each one receives the same treatment. If not you may be deemed a bad boss.

Exploitation

On company-related automobile trips, do you always make employees drive? My boss in my first management consulting firm literally gave me responsibility for all clients beyond a thirty minute drive, irrespective of the nature of the work or my ability to handle the assignment. Little wonder why my car averaged 25,000 miles per year and I was always exhausted. Do you require your staff to commit personal time and resources in executing tasks that you're not willing to commit yourself in handling your responsibilities? If so, you may be creating a work environment in which employees feel that they're being exploited.

Granted, as supervisor or boss with far greater responsibility than that of any employee whom you supervise, it is important to optimize or effectively allocate scarce resources—namely, your time—while on the job. However, if you establish a standard which you personally do not live up to or you devise policies to facilitate disproportionate convenience for yourself you may soon find yourself on the "bad boss list."

Offering the Continuing Promise

A frequent trap that many supervisors fail to avoid is offering a continuing promise to employees. By continuing promise, I mean the hint or outright declaration that a more favorable future is in store for some or all of your staff if they accomplish X,Y,Z.

Offering a promise to employees in and of itself is not necessarily a bad management practice. Offering a continuing promise, i.e., one that is not fulfilled but reoffered after original goals or favorable outcomes have been reached does reflect poor management. That should be avoided at all costs.

Ask yourself, "Do I habitually make promises to employees that I don't keep or that I can't keep on time?" It is far better not to promise anything, than to break or not keep a promise. One exceptionally effective supervisor lived by what might be a familiar credo—**"Never promise more than you can deliver, always deliver more than you promised"**.

The Dangling Carrot

Closely related to continuing promise is the dangling carrot. Do you find yourself asking more of employees just before they're due for a raise or a vacation? This is a form of coercion which many employees find aggravating or worse, bitterly resent.

The good supervisor attempts to maintain an even keel and a balanced workload for employees throughout the year and doesn't resort to cornering employees at opportune times.

Light Use of Heavy Terms

Some supervisors get in the habit of adopting management or corporate buzz words to try to motivate staff but really don't believe in or practice the declaration being made. For example, do you urge your staff to show loyalty to the department or organization while displaying none yourself? Do you ever count on or ask for the friendship of employees while not truly being a friend at all?

Use of these terms and other high-minded terms or concepts such as "commitment," "teamwork," "team spirit," and "dedication," mean very little spoken to employees when they are actually outside the bounds of your own management style. If you find yourself resorting to platitudes when supervising employees, there's a good chance of turning them off.

Programming for Failure

A particularly loathsome practice is to program your staff for failure. This is characterized by making assignments that can't be completed successfully or by not providing sufficient guidance or resources that would assist the successful completion of the task

150

assigned. Smart employees know when they've been programmed for failure and hopefully take action to obtain the guidance or resources needed before a crucial deadline is missed or an important project botched.

If you're in the habit of doling out assignments that have built-in time bombs, you'll quickly develop a poor reputation.

Throwing Curve Balls

When you communicate with your staff, do you throw curve balls—that is, alter the meaning of something that you said previously? Poor supervisors are in the habit of "bending" what was assigned or said to suit their own current need. That same boss that gave me all the long road trips also had the nasty habit of changing instruction in mid-stream and vehemently denying that any change had been made from the original instructions. Have you ever felt like wanting to tape someone to catch them in his/her own inconsistency? Believe me, I have wanted to.

If you find yourself continuously saying to employees "that's not what I said" or "that's not what I meant," you may be a curve-ball pitcher without knowing it. A curve-balling supervisor is particularly troublesome for employees who are often not at liberty to explain to you your error or to challenge your method of giving and following up on assignments.

Fixed in Stone

The flip side of being a curve-ball pitcher is being overly rigid when issuing assignments or maintaining work schedules. In the changing work place in the society of the 80's many employees have needs for flexibility in both the hours that they work and the order in which assignments are due.

The supervisor who arbitrarily clings to traditional schedules that are not based on any true organization, department or personnel needs will be quickly deemed inflexible by the staff.

Zero Feedback

Are you in the habit of informing your staff of department or organizational developments only when the news is good or when it's convenient or advantageous for you to do so? One is reminded of the story about a twelve-year-old who had never spoken in his whole life. His parents took him to doctors, but no one could find anything wrong. One morning his mother burned the toast and overcooked the eggs at breakfast. Whereupon the young man jumped up from the table and said, "This breakfast is terrible." His parents were aghast and asked why he had never spoken before. The boy replied, "up till now everything had been okay!"

Employees have a right to learn of developments which may impact upon their jobs or performance. Some supervisors, however, provide or withhold information as it suits the supervisor and not necessarily as is needed to foster an atmosphere of trust and cooperation.

Employees need to hear of negative developments as well as positive ones. Granted, this does not mean that you are duty or honor bound to instantly report to your staff everything that occurs. However, if you maintain a policy of consistently withholding information from your staff, particularly when they end up gaining at least partial information from secondary sources the "bad supervisor" tag will soon be on you.

It's Your Choice

One can choose to appease employees or latch on to what's popular to avoid being labeled a bad boss. However, there is a more important reason for you as supervisor to avoid the bad boss designation and that is that your ability to work with, motivate and further develop your staff will be directly related to the respect and feeling that your staff has for you. Therefore, from a purely pragmatic standpoint, a good supervisor must balance what he/she wants to do, knows is right, and knows will enhance the greatest long-term department or organizational benefit.

Here's an important checklist of behavior to avoid:

- [ ] Being **unfair or inconsistent** to one employee
- [ ] **Requiring more** of your staff than you'd do or have done
- [ ] Offering a **continuing promise**
- [ ] **Tempting an employee** with a "carrot" before raise time
- [ ] **Using terms** you don't follow or believe in
- [ ] **Programming** your staff **for failure**
- [ ] Retracting what you said, or altering it later—**"curveballing"**
- [ ] Being **inflexible**
- [ ] Providing little or **no feedback** (see Chapter 24)

The next chapter challenges your listening capability—something on which we all can improve.

CHAPTER TWENTY-FOUR
FAILING TO LISTEN

Listening is such a rare commodity in society that the Sperry Corporation effectively built its image by positioning itself as "the company that listens." According to researchers at the University of Minnesota, on the average, people spend 45 percent or nearly half of their communication time listening. Good listening is an active, complex process that requires knowing a few basic tenets and lots of practice. In a personal or professional relationship, it pays for both to sharpen listening skills.

Few managers/supervisors, or people in general for that matter, have thought about **learning** how to become a good listener. We get distracted when someone is talking, jump ahead in our minds to what we want to say next, and later blame the speaker for not getting the message across.

Let's learn how to become better listeners or, as fellow speaker and trainer Lou Hampton says, to "listen legibly." This chapter will provide answers to the following:

- □ What does **active listening** involve? (Hint: a one word answer)
- □ **Why don't we listen** as well as we could, and should?
- □ If you **"drop out "** of a conversation are you likely to catch up later?
- □ How much **faster can we think** than speak?
- □ What is the most positive, rewarding combination of non-verbal **responses that we can offer** a speaker?
- □ Does **location** affect our listening capacity?

Listening Involves Work

Dr. Mortimer Adler of the Aspen Institute, in his highly respected book *How to Speak and How to Listen*, says active listening involves work. Though listening occupies more of our time than speaking or reading, Adler says, we seldom receive any training in this area.

Why don't we listen as well as we should? Dr. Chester L. Karrass, Director of the Santa Monica, California based Center for Effective Negotiating, offers several reasons:

★ **We often have a lot on our minds** and it's not easy to switch gears quickly to fully absorb and participate in what is being said to us.

★ We have adopted the habit of talking and **interrupting** too much and do not let the other party continue even when it may be to our benefit.

★ We are **anxious to rebut** what the other person has said, and if we do not do so readily, we are afraid that we may forget to make our point.

★ We allow ourselves to **be easily distracted** because of the setting or environment in which the meeting takes place. Have you ever asked your secretary to hold all phone calls during meetings?

★ We **jump to conclusions** before all the evidence has been presented or is available.

★ We **discount or "write-off" some statements** because we don't place importance on the party who is presenting them.

★ We tend to **discard information** that doesn't match what we want to hear or that we don't like.

Dr. Karrass points out that "poor listeners often drop out of a conversation in the hope that they will catch up later. This seldom happens." If you find your mind wandering away while listening, make a conscious (and repeated, if need be) effort to focus on the conversation.

You're Not Alone

If by now, you've confessed to yourself that you're not a good listener, lighten up—you do not have a monopoly on underdeveloped listening skills. Virtually all human beings, especially supervisors, must work to improve their listening skills. Because we are able to think and process thoughts four to five times faster than the normal speaking rate, it is easy to let our minds race ahead of the speaker, not focus on what is being said, or appear uninterested. The faster our ability to process information, the greater the potential for our display or practice of poor listening when an oral presentation is being made to us. Good listeners use this lag time to make mental summaries of information presented and notes of ideas to pursue later without losing focus on the conversation.

Stuart L. Tubbs, of the General Motors Institute, believes that visual cues are highly influential in interpersonal communication. Facial expression and eye contact are two of the most important visual cues. For example, if you avoid eye contact while listening, this could communicate disapproval or disinterest. Even if you look directly at someone, your facial expression may still indicate a negative reaction. Tubbs points out that "probably the most rewarding combination is a smiling face and a head nod in combination with direct eye contact."

From these and other cues we infer support, confirmation, and agreement. A good way to enhance one's listening capability is to pick a location and a time (when possible) that is free from noise and interference when listening to someone (or some media message).

Also as an exercise, try speaking to one of your staff for several minutes with a tape recorder on. Then play back the tape. You may be quite surprised as to what you missed.

Here is a checklist developed by Dr. Richard C. Cupka to help you evaluate your own listening habits:

(   ) Do you give your staff members a chance to talk?
(   ) Do you interrupt while someone is making a point?
(   ) Do you look at the speaker while he/she is speaking?
(   ) Do you impart the feeling that your time is being wasted?
(   ) Are you constantly fidgeting with a pencil or paper?
(   ) Do you smile at the person talking to you?
(   ) Do you ever get employees off the track or off the subject?
(   ) Are you open to new suggestions or do you stifle them immediately?
(   ) Do you anticipate what the other person will say next? Do you jump ahead anticipating what his/her next point will be?
(   ) Do you put the employees on the defensive when you are asked a question?
(   ) Do you ask questions that indicate that you have not been listening?
(   ) Do you try to out-stare the speaker?
(   ) Do you overdo your show of attention by nodding too much or saying yes to everything?

(   ) Do you insert humorous remarks when the other person is being serious?

(   ) Do you frequently sneak looks at your watch or the clock while listening?

This is a tough checklist and anyone who is honest with him/herself will undoubtedly discover several areas for improvement. Becoming an active and effective listener provides two other important benefits:

★ You may gain information from new sources that previously would have been missed due to poor listening.

★ Even if you don't agree with the other person, at least he/she will feel that you gave them a fair shake.

Developing good listening habits is one way to become a better communicator. Active listening improves your interpersonal skills and human relations capabilities. Good listening can enhance your personal and professional life. The sooner you start listening effectively, the better. You hear!

To summarize, good listening:

☐ **takes work**
☐ means not **"dropping out"** and trying to catch up later
☐ is a universally **rare** capability
☐ **can be exhibited** by smiling, nodding and looking at the speaker
☐ is enhanced by a **location** free from noise and interference
☐ **helps develop** our overall communication capabilities

Another pitfall to avoid is not keeping your staff informed of both good and bad news that may be of concern to them. Chapter Twenty-Five, "Practicing Paternalistic Supervision" deals with this issue.

CHAPTER TWENTY-FIVE

PRACTICING PATERNALISTIC SUPERVISION

Despite breakthroughs in management theory, the paternalistic supervisory manager can still be found stalking the corridors of business and industry. The paternalistic supervisor tends to treat his/her staff like children. While it is necessary and recommended to inform employees of both good and bad developments within the organization, the paternalistic supervisor will often provide information only on good developments, shielding employees from news or information that is deemed less than good.

This chapter expands on the "zero-feedback" portion of Chapter 22. After finishing this chapter, you'll gain answers to the following:

- ☐ **Why do some supervisors avoid** disseminating information on bad developments?
- ☐ What does **"telling it like it is"** gain for the supervisor?
- ☐ How can you **squelch rumors** and reduce speculation quickly?
- ☐ What **might you get** after disseminating the news? (Hint: one word answer)

Give yourself a Chance

In observing the phenomenon of the paternalistic supervisor, the story comes to mind of the teacher who is told on the first day of school that the students this semester are slow learners and lack enthusiasm. After but a few minutes in the class on the first day, sure enough, the teacher confirms the original report. Such is the case with the paternalistic supervisor.

If the supervisor believes that his/her employees are not able to accept and handle both good information and bad, then the same situation is being created as was done in the classroom example. The teacher who treats the students as slow learners with no enthusiasm never really knows the learning capacity of the students and their potential for enthusiastic response given a proper learning environment. Likewise, the supervisor will not know if employees can handle information on bad developments because he/she has never disseminated such information and given the employees a chance to respond.

Many supervisors will argue that disseminating information on bad developments does more harm than good. This is simply not so—if handled properly, a wide variety of benefits may be derived by the supervisor, the employees, and the organization. Moreover the danger of not relating the bad news, or misinforming, generally propagates rumors and overreaction on the part of the employees, which can create unnecessary harm and anxiety. Many an inaccurate rumor has leaked out of companies, often onto the business pages of the local newspaper, all because some highly misinformed (or worse, never informed) employee came to some outrageous conclusion and then overreacted.

What are the benefits of treating employees like adults—of informing them of both good and bad developments of the company? Let's examine them in detail.

Gain Respect

When employees are treated like adults and given information that is of importance to their careers and well-being, the supervisor gains respect. In an era of oversell, overpromise, and underdeliver, employees respect the candor of a supervisor who is able to "tell it like it is," and who goes easy on the sugar coating. In one plant in the sunbelt, a supervisor was able to gain the respect and cooperation of his staff by temporarily shifting to a 4-day work week, with commensurate reduced pay, instead of having to lay anyone off.

Rolling with the Punches

Providing employees with adverse information helps prepare them to develop a framework for rolling with the punches. Over time, they will come to realize that some bad company news is part and parcel to being in business and must be taken in the proper context. The organization has undoubtedly survived time and time again, and employees soon come to realize that bad news and bad developments are often temporary.

Part of the Team

Employees who are treated like adults and are provided accurate, relevant information from their supervisors and upper management tend to feel more like part of the team (also see Chapter 18) trusted members of the company, and equals in mature response to adverse situations. Noted team productivity and team building specialist Robert Bookman, president of Bookman Resources has encouraged and observed the development of this phenomenon many times. "Office mates," says Bookman, "who feel like they're part of the same team, tend to develop a collective 'we can handle it' attitude."

Less Down Time

The fastest way to squelch rumors, reduce speculative conversation on the state and direction of the company, and get people back into a productive mode is to provide the facts as they develop.

It is ironic that most managers have a hard time facing employees when bad news must be disseminated. Yet this is the very time at which management must exhibit its ability to lead. It is easy to present good news, but it takes guts to present bad news.

Less Bitterness

In those cases when the news is very bad and includes layoffs, the supervisor or manager who has kept employees abreast of organizational developments will encounter far less bitterness and resentment if, in fact, some employees must be laid off. If this does not seem like a significant benefit, rest assured that if the time comes when you must lay off employees, having kept them informed will be of tremendous benefit.

A Chance to Prepare Intelligently

One very good reason why employees must be kept informed is that they deserve a chance to prepare intelligently for at least short-term developments within the organization. Many people don't like surprises of any nature, let alone of ill fortune. For those supervisors who are concerned that informing employees of bad developments may cause unnecessary anxiety, wasted time, etc., consider how much anxiety and wasted time will occur if news is in the form of rumor or innuendo, or how much time will be lost if management drops an information bomb and expects employees to carry on as if they had been informed all along.

A Chance to Help

Finally, and this is by far the most important benefit of informing employees of company developments, consider the tremendous pool of human resources that your employees represent. Through their collective capabilities (whatever developments are currently plaguing the company, and hence necessitating the need to present bad news), the employees may, through greater productivity, suggestions, volunteerism, or other methods, help to bring about a solution.

Witness the strong employee support at Delta, Chrysler and the Dana Corporation as chronicled by Peters, Waterman, and Iacocca. This possibility is, in itself, sufficient reason to let your employees know about company developments and to treat them like adults.

Here's a chapter wrap-up of the benefits gained by avoiding paternalistic supervision:

☐ Gain **respect** of employees
☐ Develop a team that can **roll with the punches**
☐ **Reduce** down time
☐ **Reduce bitterness**—if very bad news is forthcoming
☐ Provide employees a better **chance to prepare**
☐ Induce **staff support**.

Now let's read Chapter 26 to see what harm takes place by issuing later afternoon assignments.

CHAPTER TWENTY-SIX
ISSUING LATE AFTERNOON ASSIGNMENTS

Albert Harrison was a good, fast worker. His ability to manage his staff and turn out well crafted, voluminous weekly reports and other documents was marvelled at by all—all except the word processing department. You see, Albert's timing was atrocious. At any minute of the day, including the last one, he was likely to unload his work.

Unless you have tasks to assign that simply must be completed by the next morning, it is an unwise policy to issue assignments after 4:00 P.M. on a workday. If the assignment you must issue is of an emergency nature, then of course, any time of day will have to be sufficient for handling the emergency. However, for non-emergency and non-urgent work, issuing a new assignment to an employee late in the day can only cause problems in the long run, and reduce your credibility as a capable supervisor.

In this chapter we'll examine some of the reasons why issuing an assignment late in the day is undesirable. Specifically, these questions will be answered:

- ☐ What is the **immediate impact** on most employees receiving a late afternoon assignment?
- ☐ What does frequently issuing late afternoon assignments **indicate**? (Hint: two word answer)
- ☐ Why is the practice **ill-timed** from a productivity standpoint?
- ☐ Name some **desirable alternatives**
- ☐ What should you bestow upon any **staff member who successfully executes** your late afternoon assignments?

163

Ladies and Gentlemen, Start Your Day!

Most employees have their day planned, whether informally or formally, and receiving a new assignment within thirty to sixty minutes before departing can disrupt whatever order and serenity they have finally achieved in accomplishing whatever they had accomplished up until 4:00 P.M.

Many days, your staff may be so busy that issuing a new task late in the afternoon can only add to the tension and strain that had already been developing. Other times when your employees may not be fully occupied, the issuance of a late afternoon assignment can be met with mild panic.

It should be stressed, that by all means, employees have the responsibility to faithfully perform their duties and to follow the direction of their managers or supervisor. However, each employee likes to feel that he/she had some semblance of control of the work environment. Doling out an assignment to someone late in the afternoon shatters any precept of control that an individual may have.

Directly related, issuing late afternoon assignments may yield a pronounced increase in an employee's anxiety and can induce long-term insecurity about the working environment. We all need psychic space and time in order to perform adequately. Being summoned into the manager's office late in the afternoon and told of new and added responsibilities increases the anxiety of most employees.

Obviously, some employees thrive on activity and are eager to tackle new assignments at any time of the day or night. In your own organization you are probably already cognizant of who these people are and how to best utilize them. For the majority, however, doling out assignments after 4:00 P.M. serves no good purpose and will eventually undermine your effectiveness as a supervisor (also see Chapter 11, "Supervising Cycles of Productivity").

Is This Necessary?

Examining the issue from a supervisory standpoint, if the assignment you are issuing is of a non-emergency or non-urgent nature, then assigning it in the late afternoon can indicate poor planning on your part. This is particularly true if you know that the employee to whom you are assigning this new task is already immersed in another project that will not conclude for at least several days.

Many employees, justly or unjustly, also believe that the supervisor who doles out assignments late in the afternoon is demonstrating poor planning and/or supervisory skills. Thus, late assignments are often received and completed with a slight tone of resentment on the part of the employees receiving such assignments.

How Much Can Really Be Accomplished?

A very important question you should ask yourself before doling out a non-urgent, late afternoon assignment is, how much can really be accomplished on the day the assignment is issued? Can an employee who is about to depart in thirty or sixty minutes adequately comprehend new instructions for completing this assignment, read any available literature, or make any in-roads towards completion?

For most people, as pointed out earlier on page 77, productivity is generally highest in the morning and is understandably lower in the late afternoon of the working day. Thus, from a productivity standpoint, it makes poor (if any) sense to dole out assignments late in the afternoon unless it is absolutely necessary. In general, employees will be less motivated, more fatigued, and less likely to plunge into the new assignment with vigor.

In issuing an assignment late in the afternoon, what could be your real objective? Do you, as supervisor, feel a pressing need to get things off your desk and on to the desk of others? Do you sincerely believe that a half hour or hour that an employee may be able to expend on a new assignment will be the most effective and efficient use of his or her time? That same boss who sent me on the longest trips also made a point of loading me up (down!) with assignments in the last 3 minutes of the day before my vacations! Think twice before handing out those late afternoon assignments and the operations of your plant or division may run smoother in the long run.

Desirable Alternatives

While it is not recommended that assignments be issued late in the afternoon, it is entirely recommended that assignments be **introduced**, to be **started** the **next day**, later in the week or some time in the immediate future.

In this respect, the employee can be "oriented" in the right direction and be able to integrate this new assignment into his/her plans. You may provide or suggest background material to read or analyze, sources of information including phone numbers to call or individuals to write to.

It is helpful to provide a rough outline (as discussed in Chapter 13) or working plan on how the assignment is to be handled, with mention that this will all be discussed again later in more detail.

It is also recommended that you do **ask** an employee if he or she can handle a quick assignment or if he/she can restructure his or her plans on short notice to add this assignment to other professional responsibilities. Most good employees, when asked to take on an additional assignment late in the afternoon, will respond **affirmatively** as they are often eager to show the boss a willingness to make the extra effort, or they actually do have sufficient slack time in which the new assignment can be handled or initiated.

Praise'm to the Hilt

Finally, be sure to give **lavish praise** to any employee who successfully handles late afternoon assignments. This will help to reduce an employee's anxiety about receiving such assignments in the future and will help create an environment where if necessary (or even if not necessary for that matter) you will be able to successfully issue late afternoon assignments periodically.

In the long run, avoiding the issuance of new assignments late in the afternoon will be best for everyone.

Here's a checklist of solid reasons for avoiding issuing late afternoon assignments:

- ☐ **disrupts** employees' personal cycles
- ☐ adds to employees' **stress** and anxiety
- ☐ is **not** often **necessary**
- ☐ is **perceived as poor supervision** and/or planning
- ☐ may **not** yield **adequate** return
- ☐ is **contrary to peak** productivity periods.

If you can't avoid issuing late afternoon assignments, here's a summary on how to handle it best:

- ☐ offer the assignment as an **introduction**
- ☐ supply **supporting** materials
- ☐ **ask employees** if they can absorb a new assignment
- ☐ offer **lavish** praise

Now let's look at the insidious habit of assigning or monitoring employees outside of the office in Chapter 27.

CHAPTER TWENTY-SEVEN

MANAGING OUT OF THE OFFICE

Jim Roberts had come into work early one morning so that he could finish up a project that required a few final touches. By 11:30 a.m., Jim had accomplished a great deal as the project was completed that morning. Near lunch time, Jim took the elevator down to the main floor and was about to cross the block to get a sandwich when he passed his boss, Ed Simmons.

Ed was preoccupied in thought and hadn't really noticed Jim when he passed by with a big "hello." Ed managed to say, "Hi, Jim" and then proceeded on for but a few steps, when he turned around and said in a louder voice, "Say, Jim." Jim then retreated into the main lobby to hear what Ed had to say.

"I've got some figures I'd like you to check, and also the Walker Company report from last month should be revised, and also blah, blah, blah. . . ."

Is this scene all but too familiar? In this chapter we'll answer these questions:

- ☐ How **widespread** is managing/supervising out of the office?
- ☐ Why do supervisors **frequently commit** this sin?
- ☐ Is supervising out of the office a **timesaver**?
- ☐ How do collared employees **feel**?
- ☐ Why is it **harmful** for a supervisor to always be Mr. or Ms. Business?

Let's continue now with what happened between Ed and Jim.

I Can't Hear You

By this time, Ed finished his monologue. What he was saying really didn't matter too much to Jim. You see, Jim had put in a good morning's work and was now on his way to lunch, and while he would normally be ready to tackle any assignment given him, at this particular moment he was simply not interested.

When Ed finally finished, Jim almost inaudibly muttered, "Okay, just gotta grab a bite to eat." He then made his way to one of the sandwich shops with about one-tenth of the enthusiasm of several minutes ago.

This situation, unfortunately, occurs thousands of times every working day. Ed and Jim have a fairly sound working relationship and it is not Ed's intention to demoralize Jim. Nevertheless, discussing assignments and responsibilities during chance meetings in the lobby of the building or the sandwich shop is of no benefit to anyone.

Why does an otherwise professional, well meaning supervisor often forget that there is a proper time and place to discuss work assignments and job responsibilities and that the discussion of either of the above at the wrong time or place can demotivate or dampen the spirits of the most loyal and hardworking of employees?

Many Reasons

One reason why a well-meaning supervisor may inadvertently and inappropriately "collar" an employee outside of the office or on otherwise "neutral" ground, is that he/she simply happens to think of the task at the moment he/she was passing an employee and didn't wish to lose that particular train of thought. Occasionally, we all have thoughts for which we feel we'll forget if unless we express them immediately.

For the supervisor, however, discussing or issuing an assignment on the spur of the moment can only reflect poor planning. The actual number of times when a particular employee must be informed of a task or a responsibility on neutral ground is, in fact, minimal. Assuming the employee is doing his or her job, and the manager has effectively coordinated planning responsibilities, no employee should have to be collared in the lobby or washroom unless there is a company emergency, or unless the supervisor has ample justification for doing so.

Some supervisors who practice such a technique mistakenly believe that discussing an assignment in the stairwell is a time saver. Nothing could be further from the truth; most employees will not be mentally prepared to hear your message. Thus, if you provide instructions at the wrong time, you're likely to have to repeat them.

If I had a nickle for every time I encountered someone doling out instructions to someone else in the mens room, I still wouldn't get rich. But the scene is frequent, and if it weren't so aggravating would be comical.

Often, supervisors who give instructions outside of the office proper may do so because they believe it is part of their job, or consistent with the role that they must maintain. This belief is also fraught with illusion; always appearing as Mr. or Ms. Business to those that one must supervise establishes a superhuman standard which ultimately cannot be maintained. There is nothing wrong with letting employees know that you are human, that you do not think solely about business all day long, and that you possess the ability to "come down from the mountain" at least occasionally.

Nothing Else to Say?

Many supervisors who dole out assignments at inappropriate times engage in such action because they have nothing else to say even though they recognize that this behavior is not recommended. This is a tragedy of interpersonal communication. If, when passing an employee whom you supervise, you can think of nothing else to say besides "The XYZ report has to go out next Tuesday," then you are in serious trouble.

If you are at a loss for words when passing an employee, you might try commenting on the weather that day, praising an article of the employee's clothing, or just plain saying, "hello" and leaving it at that. If the "cat" has really got your tongue, you can even just nod or smile—anything but resort to the retreat of playing supervisor in the streets.

Finally, supervisors who dish out assignments in the main lobby are totally insensitive to the employee. These supervisors may think, "Oh, it's okay," or "Joe Smith takes everything in stride," or, "Sally knows that I know she's a good worker." These assumptions are simply unfair. It is important to remember that as supervisor, your words hang heavy on an employee's mind. William A. Marstellar said it best in *Creative Management*: "Everyone who works for you is afraid of you to one degree or another." For you to discuss a task in the elevator might indicate to the employee that the task is of considerable importance, that the employee has not been effective lately, or that something else is wrong.

How Do They Feel

From an employee's perspective, being given an assignment at the wrong time can contribute to an atmosphere of constant pressure. An employee may soon feel that there are not even minor periods of rest on the job; just push, push, push for greater efficiency or higher productivity. The employee who feels that he or she is always "under the gun," will start to be absent more often, will not volunteer for as many tasks as before, or may begin to prolong present tasks. I once surveyed several dozen people on this issue and **no** one likes it, although a few said its was okay, occasionally.

Many employees will believe that you are insensitive to their needs. It is both **helpful** and **necessary** that some moments of the work week not be filled with new instructions. Many times after an employee has put in a good morning's work and is heading for lunch, the noon break becomes much more important to him or her than otherwise. It is not merely a time for nourishment; it is also a time to psychologically readjust to forthcoming tasks and responsibilities.

In one sense a lunch break, upon completion of an important project, can even serve as a vacation which provides nearly the same benefits as an actual week-long vacation.

Care to know what an employee will think of you if you maintain the practice of collaring him or her on neutral turf? He or she is eventually bound to believe that you lack the fundamental skills of a supervisor. If employees are already aware of the project or task that you are discussing, they may also believe that you are absent-minded or at least forgetful.

Another strong reason why one shouldn't manage in the streets is that it is **patronizing**. Have you ever gotten into an elevator where a supervisor apparently was giving instructions to an employee as the elevator proceeded to the ground floor at the close of a work day? It is not a particularly exhilarating scene, and almost makes one want to say, "Enough, save it for tomorrow" directly to the supervisor.

In Summary

To review:

☐ avoid **giving instructions,**

☐ issuing **new assignments**, and
☐ reminding employees of responsibilities **while** on the street, in the lobby, riding the elevator, or in the washroom
☐ strive to **avoid** these practices first thing in the morning, near lunchtime, or late on Friday.

You'll be perceived as a better supervisor and your interpersonal communications will improve. Most importantly, however, your employees will be better motivated and happier.

Now, let's look at a modern day phenomenon among supervisors, the would-be Lou Grants.

CHAPTER 28

PLAYING WOULD-BE LOU GRANTS

Would-be Lou Grants picture themselves as the tough but lovable "Lou Grant" character on TV. Ed Asner developed a two edged character with depth that many of us have come to know well. He can be a man's man; tough, hard and mean when the situation merits it. And Lou can always make the right decision at the right time. He is authoritative and a source of strength to his employees.

But, the reason why Lou was so appealing to America's audiences is that he was also understanding, and compassionate. He could be sympathetic, comforting and there when you needed him. He was a good listener and a warm being. It's easy to like a boss who blends compassion and toughness so well.

Lou Grant is lovable and cute like a teddy bear, and tough like a grizzly bear.

What, then, is a would-be Lou Grant? This brief chapter will tell you.

What is a Would-be Lou Grant?

Visibly, it's usually a supervisor with a staff of 6 to 12. Would-be's do want their employees to love and respect them. However, because they have no idea how to act to achieve this closeness they've copied someone they admire.

Unfortunately, the idolization and emulation rarely succeeds. The Would-be Lou Grant comes on too strong and too hard, with little true compassion for anyone. He doesn't realize that true great strength is evidenced by the abilities to listen sympathetically and to be "soft" at the proper times.

As an interviewer, Would-be Lou Grants will tell you when they hire you, "I'm tough but I'm fair. You work for me and I'll work for you. I can be very understanding." If these words are true, the employee is lucky to be working for a real Lou Grant type. But all too often the Would-be Lou is 99% tough, and 1% understanding.

Would-be Lou Grants never seem to understand that real strength can also be exhibited by showing warmth and or being compassionate. Would-be's perceive themselves as two-sided persons, but in fact only have the guts to be tough. They don't have the guts to be gentle. Yet ironically and sadly, their self-perception is that of the well rounded person they'd like to be.

As a supervisor, Would-be Lou Grants assume their employees really do want to be advised on personal problems. However, no employee eats lunch with, or invites Would-be Lou Grants to go to happy hour; they've already heard enough during the workday. Would-be Lou Grants think they're close to their employees and associates by holding court the first half hour every Monday while talking football and giving excellent quarterback hindsight advice.

Would-be Lou Grants confuse "getting involved " with butting into conversations when they're not wanted. Also, they like to give short answers to involved questions. When someone does ask, "What should I do Lou?" they reply with answers like, "Set up a meeting," "send a memo," "set a deadline."

Real Lou Grants both encourage and motivate their staffs. Would-be's are too negative about themselves to believe strongly in others. Instead of extending an unreasonable deadline, Would-be's come on "tough" with statements such as, "Stay late if you have to," or "Hell, we're paying you to produce so, produce."

Would-be Lou Grants invariably have bad timing because they usually don't understand the mood of the moment. Because they are not interested in their employees they are insensitive to their needs. Would-be's think most of the "psyche" and "get your head on straight" books are for the birds.

The Would-be Lou Grant's greatest joy is proclaiming: I have a great relationship with my people because I listen to them and understand their problems."

CHAPTER TWENTY-NINE

UNDERMINING THE IDEAL EMPLOYEE

Wendy Hughes works long and hard. She gets things right and is an employee who can be relied upon. Why would Wendy encounter significant problems as a result of her efforts?

Do you supervise an "ideal" employee, someone who comes to work on time, willingly puts in overtime, does what is delegated to him or her, always gives 100%, and often a little more, is loyal and a definite asset?

Often the employee that follows the boss' requests diligently, shows loyalty, doesn't participate in the employee scuttle-butt, and consistently puts in a full day's work, arouses the jealousy and suspicion of co-workers and the **supervisor**! Regardless of the "ideal" employee's intentions, many are ready to believe that the employee is an "apple polisher" or a "brown noser."

In this chapter we will explore the supervisory pitfall of contributing to the undermining of an ideal employee, and answer the following:

- ☐ What are some of the reasons why **supervisors** may be suspicious of ideal employees?
- ☐ Why are **co-workers suspicious**?
- ☐ How do **salary problems** foul up good employees?
- ☐ Do ideal employees get **taken for granted**?
- ☐ What is the **Persian Messenger Syndrome**?

Suspicious Supervisors

Believe it or not, many supervisors are suspicious of an ideal employee and are, in fact, actively seeking "clues" as to why the employee is doing such a good job. The supervisor may have known or worked with a previous employee who also exhibited a

175

high achievement level and sound fundamental business skills, only to learn that this person

(1) was preparing to start a business of their own,
(2) was using the experience to attain a new better paying job in another firm or
(3) was camouflaging their real interests which were contrary to the objectives of the organization.

Thus as the "ideal" employee continues to work harder to impress his or her boss, a greater degree of suspicion may ensue. There are also many employees that do not give a full day's work, who do not follow their supervisor's requests, and who are not willing to give their "all." When they encounter someone that does an outstanding job, defense mechanisms don't allow them to believe that the "ideal" employee is, in fact, doing an excellent job.

Since in most businesses, cooperation and team work is needed to produce a synergistic effect that leads to success, the ideal employee, (because of subtle ways that co-workers practice ostracism), often ends up doing many tasks alone or concluding that it would be easier to go his or her own route in completing projects. Thus, the unobservant supervisor may regard the employee as "not a good team member."

Underpayment

The ideal employee naturally assumes that he or she can look forward to an uninterrupted, increasing stream of earnings. They have been, after all, highly efficient and effective in contributing to the total profitability of the firm.

A problem can result when it's time for a raise and the employee, knowing full well how hard he or she has worked feels "gypped" when the increase is less than expected. The supervisor, on the other hand, may feel that the increase in the employee's compensation has been fairly determined. Thus, an ideal employee may be "ideal" only for a time; time being defined as that period in which he or she is earning income commensurate with the contribution.

Exploitative Supervisor

Far too often, an ideal employee is exploited by the supervisor. This is characterized by increasing assignments, without increasing recognition of the waving of the proverbial "carrot" (see Chapter 23) for an extended period, or negating or not properly recognizing continuing contributions that the employee has made.

All of the above can also be viewed as "taking the employee for granted." This is a costly mistake for supervisors in that the ideal employee is often recognized, unfortunately, after departing the organization.

One Atlanta attorney confessed (after the fact) that he had employed the world's best legal secretary and because she was so good, thought there was no end to the volume of work he could assign to her. There was an end—she departed for the same pay under less exploitive circumstances.

Under-Utilization

Sometimes an employee is so good on the job that the chances for increased responsibility are diminished because the supervisor is reluctant to make the change. Thus many "ideal" employees can often find themselves under-utilized despite doing an excellent job.

Potential Inability to Look Out for One's Self

Finally, let's examine how an ideal employee can run into trouble on the job because he or she is unskilled in self protection techniques. The Persian Messenger Syndrome is one situation that confronts many employees. The Syndrome got its name because in ancient times, the King of Persia was known to reward those messengers that brought him good news and to cut off the heads of those messengers that brought bad news. Naturally, this prompted most messengers to bring only good news.

The inherent difficulty here is that the messengers who should have been rewarded, were those that brought bad news, because it's more difficult to bring bad news. The king, of course, didn't separate the messenger from the news that he/she was bringing.

Unfortunately, the Persian Messenger Syndrome exists today in large measure throughout business and government. The ideal employee, upon preparation of a financial report or a numerical analysis may determine that the dissemination of bad news is in order.

By candidly presenting the information, or by not reducing the degree of the bad news (through careful use of descriptive adjectives,) even an "ideal" employee may be stepping on a land mine if the supervisor falls prey to the Syndrome. This is but one example of many ways an ideal employee's inability to cover him or herself can produce negative effects.

The examples cited above illustrate that through minor misunderstandings, defense mechanisms and other factors of distortion, even an "ideal" employee can run into trouble on the job.

Are you guilty of any of the following:

- ☐ Being **suspicious** of good workers?
- ☐ Supporting co-worker **ostracism**?
- ☐ Supporting an **insufficient compensation** arrangement?
- ☐ **Waving** the proverbial **carrot**?
- ☐ **Under-utilizing** and then **holding back** a key staff person?
- ☐ **Impersonating** the King of Persia?

Avoiding supervisory pitfalls, upon which section IV has focused, in many ways is the flip side of communicating with style.

In Section V which follows, starting on page 179 , we'll plunge head long into "Tackling Problems Professionally."

SECTION V

TACKLING PROBLEMS PROFESSIONALLY

In this section we'll examine some tough problems that are bound to come your way and how to tackle them professionally. Chapter 30, "Laying the Groundwork for Redress," will give you the proper perspective and action steps necessary to effectively deal with the problems discussed in the chapters that follow.

The chapters are presented in increasing order of the severity of the problems you may face through "Facing Up to the Fear of Firing," Chapter 36. Chapter 37, "Helping the Battered Employee," represents departure from the progression and examines a little discussed, frequently occurring problem in today's workplace.

As a result of completing the chapters in this section you'll gain a simple yet workable framework for handling situations that have traditionally caused supervisors the most grief.

CHAPTER THIRTY

LAYING THE GROUNDWORK FOR REDRESS

Ideally, you supervise a small staff of highly motivated, professionally oriented employees who can respond to "one minute" praisings or reprimands and who provide few real problems that require disciplinary action. Realistically, on occasion you may need to deal with significant problems such as high absenteeism, moonlighting and dishonesty.

This chapter lays the groundwork for tackling these tough problems professionally. The principles and procedures discussed here will be reemphasized in the chapters that follow.

The chances are your company or organization already has an established policy to deal with these more serious problems. However, organization policy provides little comfort when you're on the firing line daily and will most likely be the first to: identify the unacceptable behavior, approach the offending employee, and initiate or recommend action.

This chapter explores the following questions:

- ☐ Can a Policies and Procedures **handbook** ever effectively govern all employee activity?
- ☐ What is an effective approach to **gaining the confidence** of an employee whom you must discipline?
- ☐ Should a **record of infractions** be kept?
- ☐ How can you ensure that each of your employees **understand what is expected** of him or her?

An Impossible Task

No set of policies and procedures, rules or job regulations will ever effectively govern all human interaction and activity that transpires at the workplace. It is an impossible task for your company or organization to produce a document that will fairly and completely describe how to proceed in each possible instance in which an employee behaves unsatisfactorily.

More important than a thick policies handbook is the ability to assess a problem objectively, devise strategies for improving the situation, inform the employee of what is expected of him or her and the penalties for non-compliance.

Gaining Their Confidence

In Chapter 22, "Giving and Receiving Criticism," tips were offered on how and when to approach employees on problems related to job performance. Many of those tips also apply here. However, the nature of problems related to behavior and non-productive activity require more delicate, yet assured handling.

A good way to win the confidence of the offending employee is by describing the problem to him or her as **"one that you both have to work at solving."** It's best to start right in on the problem, avoiding chit-chat, and to gather information by encouraging the employee to speak. Also, avoid talking about the problem while standing—sitting reduces the chances of increased tensions or hostility. If possible, **be seated next to the employee** as opposed to across the table or desk. This also helps symbolize that you are on his or her side and decreases the possibility of confrontation. By developing an emotional bond to honest discussion, you can help to influence the employee more favorably.

A System for Constructive Discipline

By approaching the problem at hand in a professional, controlled manner you can actually increase morale rather than decrease it. This is because the employee is often well aware of his or her unacceptable behavior and perhaps dreaded the time in which they would be confronted by you or some other authority. Your demonstration of professionalism, objectivity, and understanding can be a key catalyst in the employee's decision to eliminate the inappropriate behavior and to take great steps towards improving the situation.

Here's a simple system for ensuring that problems are tackled professionally:

1. **Be certain** that any organizational policy and procedure guidelines that do exist are acknowledged by your staff.
2. Highlight or **display established policy** or your policy regarding specific activities which may be occurring, but are inappropriate or forbidden.
3. **Seek the help** of your boss or a peer to gain an added measure of objectivity and impartiality before confronting an employee.
4. Provide employees with **immediate feedback** when infractions have been made. Even small transgressions are important, because if they're not dealt with they often lead to even greater problems later.
5. **Keep a log** or chart of inappropriate behavior or activity which can serve as the necessary documentation if the situation grows worse and severe penalties are warranted, i.e. termination.
6. **Administer a reprimand or punitive action** using a stair step function—the more frequent or serious the transgression, the greater the penalty leading up to termination.

Don't Play Ostrich

Inexperienced or first-time supervisors sometimes have trouble dealing with serious personnel problems. The worst thing that can be done, however, is to pretend the problem doesn't exist or to look the other way to avoid a confrontation and the responsibility to administer corrective action.

In one of Hartford's largest insurance agencies, there is a 31-year-old employee who has been dying to get fired for the last two years. He is habitually tardy, unenthusiastic and occasionally insubordinate. His disheveled appearance and lackadaisical approach to his job are dead giveaways. Yet, no one has approached him regarding his inappropriate performance or demeanor. Talk about ostriches!

By laying the groundwork or establishing a system to deal with problems in advance, you reduce the chances of being caught unprepared to deal with the issue. By knowing company or organizational policy, by communicating what you require as supervisor and by maintaining sufficient documentation or gathering sufficient evidence on inappropriate behavior, you can dramatically limit the stress and anxiety of all concerned.

Here's a checklist for your review which highlights suggestions made in this chapter:

- [ ] Remember, **no set of written guidelines** will ever effectively govern all human interaction in the workplace
- [ ] Gain the **confidence** of individual staff members by working together to solve a problem
- [ ] Demonstrate **your professionalism** when dealing with a problem
- [ ] Devise a **simple system** for handling problems which includes highlighting policies, providing immediate feedback, keeping a log of inappropriate behavior, and administering reprimands or punitive action using a stair step function
- [ ] Don't avoid problems by playing **ostrich**.

In Chapter 31 we'll discuss a most insidious problem in scheduling for productivity—**absenteeism**!

CHAPTER THIRTY-ONE

DEALING WITH HIGH ABSENTEEISM

Today's the day you're going to accomplish great things. There are three reports that are nearing completion, two new projects to be started and you feel rarin' to go! Unfortunately, three of your eight staff members have called in sick. Now it's doubtful that very much will get done today.

Your organization's policy on absenteeism, tardiness, and reporting should be a fundamental part of the new employee orientation procedure (see Chapter 7) and laid out expressively in the policies and procedures guide. As supervisor, however, it makes sense to reemphasize this immediately prior to hiring and shortly after an employee begins work. Absenteeism is very costly, and the disruption in your department's work flow can be both aggravating and disheartening. You probably can't afford to be absent from your job. Some of your staff believe they can.

In this chapter we'll highlight what can be done at the supervisory level to effectively deal with the problem of excessive absenteeism and help you to answer these questions:

- ☐ **Who** is most often absent and why?
- ☐ Do **major sports events** contribute to absenteeism?
- ☐ What **techniques** have been proved to be ineffective?
- ☐ Are most employees surprised when they learn how they **compare** to others?
- ☐ What **six steps** effectively **combat** absenteeism?
- ☐ What is **"push"** policy?

What Do We Know About Absenteeism?

Research conducted over the last several years, reveals predictable patterns of absenteeism across a wide spectrum of business and industry. Here are eight observations that shed light on the phenomena.

- **Emotional factors** are involved in 25 percent of all absences;
- **Skilled** employees are **absent less** than unskilled or semi-skilled workers;
- Most of the absenteeism is **concentrated** in a small segment of the work population.
- Long-service, **older** employees are absent less than the "under 25" group;
- Approximately 5 percent of all one and two day absences precede or **follow** otherwise legitimate time off for holidays or weekends;
- There is a high correlation between employee "illness" and major sporting events;
- About **3 percent** of employees are practically **never absent**;
- Absenteeism increases with **prolonged overtime** and extended workweeks.

MITCH'S RELATIVES ARE DROPPING LIKE FLIES .... THIS IS THE THIRD ONE THAT'S KICKED OFF THIS MONTH . . . .

What Doesn't Work

Surprisingly, warnings to high absentee workers are seldom effective. Productivity consultant Mitchell Fein points out that the person who's absent is doing what he really wants to do—not come to work (even though he may lose wages, receive punishment, and upset productivity)—and he has the right to do what he wants. But he should do it someplace else. His personal liberty shouldn't impinge on the rights of others. Fein also maintains that efforts to reward employees to maintain good attendance has little effect, because only the good employees pick it up. Moreover, good employees still have to work harder because their co-worker fails to show up (and thus be non-productive). Responsible workers have little influence over the irresponsible to show up regularly.

What then, does work?

Reducing Absenteeism

A basic approach to reduce absenteeism is to keep good records on absences, study them to ascertain the pattern of absences, and discuss them with each employee. What are the reasons offered for being absent? Often employees are surprised when they see how their six-month record of absences compares with others.

Excessive absences and tardiness are a reflection of morale. To find the underlying causes of high absenteeism requires finding out how the offending employee views the company, his or her career, and specific assignments. Chronic absenteeism requires strong measures (see "push policy" next page).

Techniques used in various industries for reducing absences include:

★ **Avoiding paying for holidays** when an employee is absent on the day before or after the holiday;

★ **Screening** new employees closely and not hiring those with questionable attendance records at other companies;

★ Requiring that the employees must talk to their supervisor when **calling in sick**;

★ Tying **attendance** records to **promotions**;

★ Establishing a **written policy** for absenteeism, and indicating the disciplinary action which will be taken if absenteeism becomes excessive;

★ **Altering pay days** to that day in which the greatest number of employees are absent—usually Monday.

Now let's examine a strategy used by one company in Long Beach for handling absenteeism.

Push Policy

A "push" absentee policy consists of primarily three basic parts including the following:

(1) **Verbal message**—upon initial interview, before hiring, and shortly after hiring, the employee should be told the company's policy regarding absences. The employee should be told that everyone works together, that he or she is part of a team and the company or organization. The absentee policy and call-in procedure are made a **work rule**; it is a condition of employment.

(2) **Written Notice**—when an employee has been absent the supervisor must determine if the absence was excusable or not. If inexcusable, the employee should be given a written notice that only two unexcused absences will be tolerated, at the maximum. The supervisor maintains the burden of determining the true cause for the absence, and if the absence is found to be legitimately excusable to acknowledge it accordingly.

(3) **Suspension/Discharge**—if an employee has been inexcusably absent **twice** in a six month period, a face to face meeting between the supervisor and employee should be held immediately to determine if the employee should continue. Three inexcusable absences in a six month period constitutes discharge.

Does the push policy sound tough? It is. But remember, marginal employees, those that contribute the least, cause the most headaches. So, why court them?

In Chapter 32 we'll meet a type of employee who has not been absent a great deal, but might as well be.

CHAPTER THIRTY-TWO

DISLODGING THE EMPLOYEE TURNED "INSTITUTION"

Jason Woodling has been with ACME Supply for eight years. He plays golf with the branch manager's nephew and has accumulated 2 & 1/2 months of paid vacation time. Jason's voice has a commanding tone. His office is near the rear exit. And oh yeah, Jason hasn't done an honest days work in about three years.

There exists in many large organizations an employee who has effectively ceased functioning in the role or position for which he or she was originally hired, or to which the employee has been promoted. This type of employee has become what will be termed an "institution."

An employee who has become an institution within an organization is acclimated to all the ways of getting through each work day contributing as little as possible, while maintaining an appearance of being "on top" of the job.

The phenomenon of the employee turned "institution" occurs frequently throughout the federal bureaucracy since it is difficult to remove an employee from a federal position. However, business and industry also have their share (of "institutions").

In this chapter we'll take a hard look at this problem and address these questions:

☐ What are some of the **reasons** an employee becomes an institution?
☐ Why are **older employees** more likely to become institutions?
☐ What **prevailing conditions** usually exist when an employee has effectively chosen the institution route?
☐ Name four ways to **detect** an employee turned institution?
☐ What are the ways to **stop'em cold**?

188

How Does It Start?

An employee may become an institution for a variety of reasons. Sometimes the employee is related to someone in upper management, although the actual occurrence of this is minimal. Another reason is that the employee possesses specific knowledge or skills that the organization cannot readily acquire from other sources. The employee may have developed a particular expertise that, at least periodically, is of vital importance to operations.

Frequently, an employee turns "institution" within an organization simply because he or she is **allowed to**, and no one (not even the supervisor) is aware of, or willing to expose, the employee's general lack of dedication and limited effectiveness on the job.

Sometimes an older employee who has been with the organization since "way back when" can intimidate others with less seniority. Surprisingly, this intimidation may even extend to his or her supervisor.

In order for an employee to become an institution within any organization he or she has to fully "know the ropes"; he or she must be able to understand how the system works before the system can be circumvented. Hence, an employee cannot become an institution until gaining wide exposure to the system and its procedures.

Perhaps the employee worked for a time in the billing department, was transferred to sales, and then later transferred to receiving. In government, he or she may have spent time in the public relations office, acted as a special assistant to a director or worked on a special task force.

The problem of "institutions" within the ranks of the Federal Government is so pronounced that it often appears that becoming an institution is Federal employment's raison d'etre. Too bad for the rest of the country!

Usually, an employee could not turn institution without a **lack of awareness** on the part of one key supervisor or manager. In other words, there is one key person within the organization, who, with knowledge of the employee's true work habits and operating procedures, would not allow such practice to exist.

How to Spot'em

One clue that an employee has become an institution is a pronounced lack of flexibility; the employee is vitally interested in maintaining the status quo and regards change as a major enemy of the kingdom he or she has established.

The employee—turned—institution also promotes mediocrity, and when confronted with an idea from a peer or subordinate that might be good for the organization but which would also involve real work, will often respond with idea killing phrases such as "we've tried that before" or "that never works." I knew of one person who used these kinds of statements to directly ward off any new assignments or responsibilities that he might have been given.

"Institutions" are also very adept at "covering your behind" techniques and, in fact, have developed an entire set of procedures to "cover" themselves rather than truly accomplish anything for the organization. Some of the techniques used to cover oneself include faithfully filling out time sheets, completing other reporting requirements and quickly responding to memos and directives of immediate supervisors.

My least productive staff member, not coincidently, was always the first to turn in his magnificently complete timesheet.

Influence Peddling

Other ways to identify "institutions" is to observe who is influence "peddling." There is a high tendency among employees—turned—institution to influence others within the organization. Frequently, "institutions" will be leaders of employee organizations or union groups, as they often recognize that these positions will shield them from having to maintain job-related responsibility.

Many leaders of employee groups are effective as employees within the organizations for which they work. The employee—turned—institution, however, uses employee or union groups for selfish ends. He or she also seeks the loyalty of other selected subordinates and tries to form a cadre of employees that will act as a buffer to "hostile" parties.

Also, the employee—turned—institution is, more often than not, keenly aware of the benefits and deductions from his or her paycheck, and utilizes compensatory time, sick leave, and annual leave to full personal advantage. While the employee may make no significant contributions, rest assured that he/she will be well informed of organization policies and procedures, and will do what he or she can to stretch the policies for personal advantage.

How to Stop'Em Cold

The employee—turned—institution can only flourish when an otherwise good manager or supervisor refuses to see the true picture or to take corrective measures. The employee—turned—institution must be stopped cold, before he/she has a chance to:

Lower productivity,
Unfavorably influence other employees,
Demoralize other employees, or
Tarnish the organization's image to outside parties.

Once an employee—turned—institution has been uncovered, quick action must be taken. First, it is desirable to **reassign the employee** to a new department, division, or operating unit, to reduce his or her "comfort level." If the transfer is not in the best interests of the organization, then the employee should **be given new tasks** and responsibilities, while assigning previous tasks to someone else.

The employee—turned—institution should always be **physically relocated** to a different office. Preferably, the new location should be next door to you or in a highly visible spot.

Without making it obvious, you should initiate the practice of **periodically checking** to see how (or what) the employee—turned—institution is doing. If necessary, new (or expanded) daily and weekly **reporting logs** can be introduced.

Circulate a memorandum, to your staff, stating that activities and behavior that interfere with the primary functions of the group or organization will result in punitive action or dismissal. Good employees won't be troubled reading this memo; employees—turned—institution will cringe.

If an employee-turned-institution is discovered after a relatively short amount of time, sometimes a **stern message** delivered in person by you or the head of the organization can rectify the situation. However, if an employee-turned-institution has been allowed to flourish for a prolonged period, has been discovered, and the seven steps above have been ineffective, **dismissal**, unfortunately, is the best procedure. Some supervisors may find dismissal or termination too harsh. It isn't; not for someone who has **consistently circumvented the system for his/her own ends**.

Beware, the employee-turned-institution is everywhere.

Here's a review of how they get started and how to neutralize the employee-turned-institution.

How They Get Started:

- ☐ **Maintain** specific or unique skill
- ☐ Are **allowed** to
- ☐ **Related** to someone higher up
- ☐ Have been with the organization a long time, have **seniority**
- ☐ **Know** the "ropes"
- ☐ **Benefit from unaware**, intimidated or ineffective supervisor.

How To Spot Them:

- ☐ Fight to **maintain** status quo
- ☐ Promote **mediocrity**
- ☐ **Cover** themselves
- ☐ Become an **influence peddler**
- ☐ Keenly aware of **benefits** policy

How To Neutralize Them:

☐ **Reassign** to new department
☐ Assign **new tasks** or responsibilities
☐ **Relocate** them (preferably next to you)
☐ **Check** on them often
☐ Issue an **expanded reporting** form
☐ Circulate a **memo** forbidding such practices
☐ Deliver a **stern message**
☐ **Dismiss** them.

Now let's look at another insidious supervisory problem in Chapter 33—handling moonlighting on the job.

CHAPTER THIRTY-THREE

MOONLIGHTING ON THE JOB

"Employees' deliberate waste of on-the-job time cost American business over \$125 billion a year, triple the cost of shoplifting, fraud and other recognized crime" according to a 1982 study by employment specialist Robert Half. A growing portion of employees' theft of time on the job is in fact due to secondary income activities. Any secondary income activity that one of your employees engages in while on the full time job will be termed "moonlighting on the job."

There are four compelling reasons why moonlighting on the job is detrimental to your department as well as the entire organization and must be eliminated.

In this chapter these four reasons will be discussed and the following questions answered:

- ☐ How can moonlighting on the **job reduce performance beyond** the obvious loss of hours worked?
- ☐ Are moonlighters likely to engage in **conflict-of-interest** types of activity?
- ☐ What **damage** is done to your **honest** employees?
- ☐ What are some **effective guidelines** for handling moonlighting (not on the job)?

Reduces Performance

If John Clark is scheduled to work forty hours for his employer and instead devotes two hours each day to his own business, he is, in essence, providing 32 hours of work for his employer. However, the 32 hours he does provide are usually not a quality 32 hours.

In addition to the eight hours that John steals per week working on his own activity, his activity also takes up John's time at home on week nights and, perhaps, on week-ends. Thus, John's employer loses two ways:

1) by not getting a full 40-hour work week while paying for one which effectively is the same as giving John a raise in salary, and
2) by not getting quality hours for those hours that are being worked.

I UNDERSTAND HE MOONLIGHTS A LITTLE....

Use of Organization Resources

It is very likely that John, in support of his outside business activities, will use his employer's telephone, a fair amount of office supplies, copying paper and the copy machine, and maybe even postage. While it is possible to control the unauthorized use of office supplies, the control system is often much more burdensome to all. Also John's use of these resources may result in their short supply or in increased delays for those who are doing the job they were hired to do.

Conflict of Interest

John's other activity, outside of the time he's stealing from his employer and possible use of his employer's resources, may also represent a conflict of interest. If John's outside activity has nothing to do with his employer's, then perhaps this is not a problem area. However, it is reasonable to assume that John's outside activity may be a function of his principal activity and requires similar education, background and training.

Not every incidence of moonlighting on the job represents conflict of interest. However, it only takes a few that do to make a bad problem horrendous. A direct conflict-of-interest activity should be met with dismissal (see Chapter 35).

Unfair to Other Employees

Perhaps most importantly, John's preoccupation at work with outside business activities is grossly unfair to fellow employees who put in a fair eight-hours work day after day and devote their time, energy and skills to the tasks for which they were hired. Many employees who get wind of the situation may feel demoralized because John is "getting away" with something, yet they won't expose him because they don't want to "rat."

Moonlighting on the job is not restricted to marginal employees—some of the most talented, high achieving, promotable employees partake in this practice. Supervisors should not consider it an activity undertaken only by marginal employees. Everyone in the organization is a candidate.

Guidelines for Moonlighting

While **moonlighting on the job** is insidious to any organization, moonlighting per se, may not be. "Moonlighting is a natural and reasonable response to the complexity of employment and should not be swept under the table," says Thomas P. Ference, professor of management and director of the master's degree program for executives at Columbia University's graduate school of business. "It should be dealt with professionally like any other aspect of business."

If your organization hasn't established policy on moonlighting or if you need to personalize communication with your staff in this area, here are some guidelines from business and financial writer Bruce W. Fraser:

Spell out the conditions under which you approve, disapprove or will be neutral toward moonlighting. You may applaud an employee who teaches at a college or lends skills to government but disapprove of work for a firm that is in some sense a competitor.

Also state whether in-house telephones, copy machines, secretaries or computers can be used for outside purposes. Employees may, for example, be allowed to take calls related to moonlighting ventures during the day but not allowed to use a company computer or secretary in their moonlighting.

Be clear about the job performance that is expected from the employee so that both employer and employee can judge accurately whether performance is being affected by the moonlighting.

Here's a checklist on the harmful effects of not containing moonlighting on the job:

- [ ] effectively gives the culprit a **raise**
- [ ] **reduces overall performance** of and quality hours worked by the employee
- [ ] **consumes** organizational resources
- [ ] fosters **conflicts** of interest
- [ ] **demoralizes** other employees

Here are the guidelines for moonlighting policy:

- [ ] deal with it **professionally**
- [ ] **spell out the conditions** of approval and disapproval
- [ ] **cite** proper and improper use of company resources
- [ ] **spell out** expected job performance.

In the next chapter, we'll continue our look at tougher and tougher problems: employee dishonesty.

CHAPTER THIRTY-FOUR

CRACKING DOWN ON DISHONESTY

Employee theft and other dishonest behavior, which includes anything from pilfering office supplies to repeatedly using sick leave as vacation time are thought, by some, to be due to an employee's perception that the employer is not interested in his or her welfare. The sociological implications and rationale for dishonesty in the workplace are beyond the scope of this book. However, in this chapter we will explore the following questions:

★ How much does employee dishonesty **cost** American businesses each year?

★ What are the **reasons** for the persistence and universality of the practice?

★ What **can you do** to prevent employee dishonesty?

★ How can you **spot** employee dishonesty?

★ What **should you do** once you've discovered employee dishonesty in your company?

The Costs

Employee theft and dishonesty is a tough problem that doesn't go away by ignoring it. It's difficult for any manager to contemplate that his or her employees are stealing time, money, supplies, or company secrets. Once becoming aware of dishonesty among their staff, many supervisors take it as a personal affront as well as a damaging blow to the company itself. A look at some facts may convince you of the need to keep your eyes open.

A recent Department of Justice study, "Thefts by Employees in Work Organizations," estimated that the dollar loss to pilferage approaches $10 billion annually. Spread across the largest 50,000 companies in the United States, for example, this yields an average annual loss of $200,000!

Sixty percent of the retail employees who responded to a recent University of Minnesota survey report they've stolen from their companies. Many sales clerks admitted to buying goods for friends and relatives with their discount cards, while increasing numbers of buyers and managers said they're padding their expense accounts.

Retail stores are not the only place where pilferage occurs. Roughly 30 to 40% of the working population in the United States is a bad risk for handling a company's money, merchandise, and secrets. According to a Small Business Administration management aid on employee pilferage, "The trouble is that too many people take integrity for granted. Innocent until proven guilty is a meaningful and deep-rooted American principle. But it doesn't preclude the need to install effective theft deterrents and to take measures to track down dishonesty."

Security devices, no matter how effective, cannot stop the problem of employee dishonesty and cannot stop actual stealing of equipment and supplies. Strong preventive measures must be taken to deal with this problem.

Why Are Employees Dishonest?

The Department of Justice study suggests that an employee who feels mistreated is more likely to engage in "spontaneous counterproductive behavior." An employee who was discovered making as many as 30 personal, long distance phone calls using the company WATS line excused his behavior saying, "The company hadn't given me a raise in two years. Plus, the few calls I made wouldn't make one bit of difference in their expenses."

This employee didn't realize the total picture. His 30 phone calls may have taken between $100 and $200 per month from the company, now multiply that over two years, and factor in other employees partaking in the same practice, and the company could be in real trouble.

Another reason given by employees for dishonest practices is that "everybody does it, even the senior company officials." Padding invoices or switching hours from one contract to another may be seen by employees as evidence of the company's own dishonesty, giving them permission to do the same.

A report concerning several major U.S. corporations was summarized in *The New York Times*:

"Inflated expense accounts, dummy invoices for goods and services never provided and off-balance-sheet slush funds were

commonplace at companies that disguised bribes, kickbacks, political gifts, and other questionable payments on their official books and records, according to an extensive study by Charles E. Simon & Company, a Washington concern specializing in research related to Securities and Exchange Commission activities."

It's easy to see how this environment creates easy rationalizations for employee dishonesty. Your employees will know the ethical climate of the company and follow the organization's lead.

How To Prevent Employee Dishonesty

The first step in preventing employee dishonesty is to create an atmosphere of honesty and ethical behavior throughout the company. State all policies related to employee theft and dishonesty in your company policy manual along with the steps that will be taken if the rules are broken. Then be sure that the illegal, unethical methods mentioned above are not practiced in your company. Set the proper example.

Be reasonable when setting up your policies. For instance, almost every employee is going to use the photocopy machine at some time or another. Recognize this, and create reasonable limits on its use. One company allows employees to make 30 photocopies a month. If employees need more, they bring in their own paper and make up to 200 copies without charge. A minimal fee is charged for over 200 copies. The employees have an incentive to be honest, knowing that the company is making provisions for them.

Employees caught breaking the rules must be immediately disciplined, no matter how high in the company structure. Explanations for your actions should be written out in a memo or company newsletter so everyone knows the rules are being followed and punishment will occur without exception.

Saul D. Astor, president of Management Safeguards, Inc., explains why the discipline is necessary, but sometimes difficult:

"Companies are reluctant to prosecute known thieves for a number of reasons. The crook may be a personal friend of the executive he reports to. . . In some cases we run into, the manager or supervisor caught stealing is so good at his job, the CEO rationalizes that it pays to keep him on despite his dishonesty. . . . The truth is that a hardnosed attitude and policy regarding dishonesty is the only morally feasible and economically practical approach to take."

Dishonesty Should Not Be Shielded

Specific, tangible rewards can be created to encourage employees to report wrongdoing. To inspire those who would not want their names known, establish a box or area where employees can anonymously place reports on dishonesty. Create respect for the reporter, anonymous or not.

One company writes articles about its whistleblowers without mentioning names, along with detailing the amount of money the company was losing in the specific case. Does all this sound too tough? Even the Federal Government, through its GSA Fraud Hotline, is taking on the problem, head-on.

Lewis Shealy, a vice president of security for Woodward and Lothrop department stores points out several features of his security program that have proven effective:

★ Both management and sales employees, when hired, **view videotapes** of past thieves being caught.
★ Woodies offers a **substantial reward** for a report of wrongdoing that results in the conviction or dismissal of the offender.
★ It is a **condition of employment** to agree to inspection.
★ There is a generous **employee discount** program.
★ Woodies **subscribes** to an organization that tracks dishonesty in bank and retail companies by maintaining a roster and files of shoplifters and employees dismissed for dishonesty.

How To Spot Employee Dishonesty

The Loss Prevention Institute, Inc., suggests that the following clues can be uncovered in your records to help spot employee dishonesty:

CHART 19

★ Inventory records and physical counts don't match.
★ Control documents missing or out of sequence.
★ Bad checks frequently accepted or approved by one employee.
★ Unusual rise in consumption of supply items.
★ Unusually high percentage of refunds or credits.
★ Different figures on original and carbon copy of the same form.
★ Erasures, changes, or pencil entries on forms that are not supposed to be altered.

★ Substitute documents used excessively to replace "lost" records.

★ Employment record or references cannot be checked.

Signs in employee behavior or actions include:

★ Merchandise or materials missing from boxes or containers.

★ Merchandise wrapped in a bag or package for no good reason.

★ Something moved out of position between night and morning.

★ Files or documents missing or out of place.

★ Employee often carrying large bags or a stuffed briefcase.

★ A sharp rise in the number of copies made on a photocopying machine or in the number of long distance phone calls.

What to do Once You've Discovered Employee Dishonesty

After you have discovered that an employee is stealing or abusing company privileges, obtain the best proof you can. For instance, keep detailed logs, (as discussed in previous chapters), of an employee who continually comes into work late and leaves early. Have another supervisor verify this information.

Decide on the steps needed, following company policy. Does this employee deserve a probation period? (See Chapter 35) How will an immediate firing affect morale in the rest of your staff as well as overall productivity? Is a replacement readily available? These questions will also need to be addressed by you, because they'll follow closely on the heels of the action you take.

Next, call the employee into your office and confront him or her with the evidence of dishonesty. Allow the employee to explain the actions, but make clear from the start of the interview that disciplinary actions will be taken. If you have decided to fire the employee, do so immediately, remaining firm and professional. (See Chapter 36, "Facing Up to the Firing Task.")

Although you don't need to mention the disciplined or fired employee by name, use the action as reinforcement for other employees. Let them know why certain steps were taken. Be honest and forthright, and you'll retain the respect of the remaining staff.

Here is a checklist summary for the chapter:

★ Help prevent employee dishonesty by treating all employees fairly and creating an atmosphere of ethical behavior. This is **less costly and far easier** than having to detect and punish dishonesty.

★ Offer **positive reinforcement** for honest behavior and whistle-blowing on unethical employees. This is another important preventive measure.

★ **Check** all records and **monitor** employee's behavior carefully if you suspect dishonesty.

★ Obtain as much **proof** as you can of an employee's theft or abuse.

★ Mete out **punishment** that is **swift** and sure.

★ **Publicize** incidents and the resulting punishment.

Cracking down on dishonesty at all levels of your company will result in a better working atmosphere for all employees and decrease your losses.

In Chapter 35 we'll examine in further detail the steps involved in placing an employee on probation.

CHAPTER THIRTY-FIVE

PUTTING AN EMPLOYEE
ON PROBATION

Employees will not always live up to your standards or the standards of the company. Even some good employees may have periods where their work is shoddy or where they may abuse company work hours, and sick or vacation time.

This behavior creates a drain on your company's resources. Other employees must work harder to handle overflow from a poor performer and can become demoralized. You must take action immediately.

Probation (not to be confused with the mandatory probation period for all **new** employees) is defined as a trial period or the act of granting continued employment on the promise of improved behavior. It is a valuable management tool for the following reasons:

★ It gives employees **clear feedback** on their performance.
★ Correctly worded, a probation gives the employee **a goal** that is measurable and attainable.
★ It allows you to **help a good employee** over a **troubled period** without possible charges of favoritism.
★ It **minimizes the trauma** of firing, if improvement in the work or attitude doesn't occur.

Steven J. Kneeland, Ph.D., a consulting psychologist with Stevenson & Kellogg, Canadian management consultants, points out the need for an early warning system which will alert management to potential problems while there is still time to do something positive about them. Kneeland says the system should include the following elements:

★ An unambiguous and clearly agreed-upon **definition** of job responsibilities and performance expectations.

★ A regular and objective **monitoring** of actual performance against agreed-upon objectives and standards.

★ An **early signaling** of emerging problems in the form of tangible, helpful "feedback" to the individual.

★ A **review**, by the individual and the supervisor, of the various problem-solving strategies available to them.

Openly Discuss The Problem

If you notice that an employee's work is not up to standards, first check that your perception of the employee's duties and responsibilities is the same as his or hers. A recent survey showed that over half of all superiors and subordinates didn't agree on most of the subordinate's required duties.

Solve the problem by having a clear, written position description. Take the time to go over the descriptions with each employee, answering any questions they may have. Ask employees to paraphrase the list of their responsibilities to check that you agree.

Although it will be time-consuming to go through this process, it will save you time and energy when an employee doesn't fulfill his or her responsibilities.

Once you notice a decline in performance or missed hours, bring it to the attention of the employee immediately. Hoping the problem will go away by itself will only make it worse. Call the employee into your office and firmly, but professionally, state the reasons for your concern.

Always critique the behavior, not the person. "You've been at least one half hour late on 11 out of the last 12 work days. Can you explain this?" Offer the employee a precise assessment of his or her behavior, along with the opportunity for explaining it.

As indicated earlier, you should document the poor performance as specifically as possible, using dates and times when appropriate. This provides evidence if you have to fire the employee later. It also helps shape your efforts to improve the employee's performance.

This first discussion should be just that—a warning talk about the problem. Explain your judgement of the needed changes in the employee's attitude or behavior. Then ask the employee to tell you the steps he or she intends to take to affect those changes. Set a time for a review of the needed changes. Hopefully, the problem will be solved. If the employee's work does not improve, you will have to conduct a warning interview next. Summarize the discussion in a memo for your own files. Do not place a copy in the personnel file of the employee at this time.

The Warning Interview

If appropriate, ask the subordinate to evaluate his or her performance since you first mentioned a problem. Many employees will recognize and admit they have not changed. Listen carefully, praising any straightforward admissions.

Explore options with the employee at this time. Is there a poor fit between the individual and the job? Could the employee do better in another area of the company? Can the job be restructured to create a better fit? Is termination of the employee a likely option? Discuss the alternatives, taking care to listen to the employee.

Some employees may become defensive. Bring out your evidence at this turn of events. Explain that the behavior or attitude has not changed and that a memo summarizing the warning interview will be placed in his or her personnel file. Give the employee a copy of the memo.

Explain The Chain of Events

Your company policy manual should clearly define a process for dealing with poor performance. First, the discussion; next, the warning interview; then probation; and finally, if necessary, firing the employee.

This chain of events must be followed to the letter for all employees, no matter what the personal problems involved may be. Letting one employee exhibit poor performance or behavior and not taking remedial steps may lead to decreased respect for you as a manager and an increased tendency among other employees to "get away with it."

At any time, if the employee's performance has improved, point out that you appreciate the change and would like it to continue.

Probation

If the performance has remained the same, or worsened, a formal probation is called for.

A formal probation involves the following:

★ A **written record** of the performance or behavior problem.
★ A complete **list of actions** the employee must take to stay with the company.
★ A **prearranged time** for the probation period.
★ An understanding that **firing** is the only possible action **if the goals are not reached**.

Philip H. Anderson, assistant professor of management at the College of St. Thomas says, "If all else fails, the only alternative is termination. But the fired employee will know he or she was given an honest chance to succeed in the job."

The following form is an example of the documentation you need to include in a formal probation report:

CHART 20

EMPLOYEE PROBATION REPORT

Employee's Name _____

Division/Location _____

Date of violation _____ Time of violation _____

Nature of violation:

    Substandard work _____

    Conduct _____

    Disobedience _____

    Tardiness _____

    Attitude _____

    Carelessness _____

Explanation of the violation:

_____

_____

_____

Actions the employee has agreed to take during the probation period:

_____

_____

_____

Probation period: From _____ To _____

Date employee was first warned of this violation _____

```
┌─────────────────────────────────────────────────────┐
│              EMPLOYEE'S REMARKS                      │
│                                                     │
│                                                     │
│                                                     │
│                                                     │
│                                                     │
│                                                     │
│                                                     │
└─────────────────────────────────────────────────────┘
```

Employee's Signature _____ Date _____
Signature of supervisor preparing report _____
Title _____ Date _____

Here's a checklist for reaching the decision to put an employee on probation:

- [ ] Establish a **clear agreement** about the duties and responsibilities of your subordinates.
- [ ] Have an open, **warning "talk"** with an employee whose behavior or attitude is not up to par.
- [ ] If the talk was not enough, hold a **warning interview**, to be documented in the employee's personnel file. This interview should explore remedial action and support from the company for the employee to change his or her behavior.
- [ ] Follow the **chain of events** leading to probation and then firing for all employees.
- [ ] Remember, probation is a **formal action**, with a specific time period and measurable goals to be reached during this period.
- [ ] Emphasize to the employee that **firing is the only action that can be taken if the terms** of the probation **are not followed** by the employee.

If it comes down to having to fire someone, take heart, few managers or supervisors relish the thought. Far less do it skillfully. Chapter 36 will walk you through how to "face up to the firing task."

CHAPTER THIRTY-SIX

FACING UP TO THE
FEAR OF FIRING

Firing an employee is never easy. Looking someone in the face and saying that you no longer need his or her services is an emotional strain on you, on the person being fired, and can disrupt work in the rest of the organization. In fact, managers frequently postpone firing an employee, even when it is absolutely necessary, to avoid the unpleasantness.

Most supervisors/managers have little experience in firing employees and horror stories about the reactions of employees (often somewhat exaggerated) abound. Additionally, the necessity of the firing involves admitting your own prior inadequate judgement or the poor judgement of your company in hiring the person.

Done quickly, but planned thoroughly in advance, firing an employee can have some positive aspects for you, your company, and the departing employee.

If you have already decided that an employee must be fired due to poor work, a bad attitude, pilferage, or some other reason, and have followed the steps in the previous chapter on giving the proper warnings and probation, answering the questions listed below will help you face up to the unpleasant task with as little discomfort and as much benefit as possible to you, your company, and the fired employee.

- ☐ Have you **documented** the reasons for firing the employee as well as the dates and steps taken to warn him or her of poor performance?
- ☐ How is the employee's **presence affecting the morale** of the rest of the staff?
- ☐ When is the **best time** of the day and week to tell the employee?

- [ ] What **procedures** should you follow in the firing interview?
- [ ] What **positive aspects** can come for you, your company, and your former employee?

Document The Problems

As stressed in previous chapters, it is **vital** to keep a detailed record of the problems you have faced with a particular employee. Did he or she have a habit of arriving late and leaving early? Do you have written records of daily timesheets? Was the employee found stealing equipment or resources from the company? Was this documented by another person in the company or an outside agency? Was the employee's work consistently not up to par? Can another supervisor verify your comments in writing?

Keeping such a record will come in handy if you are later challenged by the former employee or a union. It will also serve as a refresher for you when preparing for the firing session.

Also keep the details on warnings and probation with the date and method written down. For instance, "John Jones was warned verbally on July 13, 1986 about his tardiness, a written warning notice (signed in acknowledgement by the employee) followed on August 1, and he was formally put on probation on August 30." This information will track the progression of events, showing that the employee was fairly and properly warned about his or her behavior and attitude, received adequate training and feedback, and had opportunities to transfer to another area of the company (if that was an option).

Recognize the Effects on Company Morale

Delaying the firing of an unproductive (and possibly destructive) employee will not make the problem go away. Other employees are often more aware than you realize of the work habits and productivity of their fellow employees. They realize when someone is "getting away with murder" and their own work may slip if they see shoddy work or work habits being tolerated.

Your staff wants to work for an effective, committed leader. They may regard your reluctance to fire an unworthy employee as evidence of your lack of respect for their good work as well as a lack of leadership. Delaying the necessary firing diminishes your professional integrity, whereas taking control of the unpleasant situation, although it may initially create some misgivings among

212

employees, will eventually result in the strong leadership employees expect and want.

John Wareham, of Wareham Associates, an executive search firm with offices around the world says, "Properly handled, done with dignity and poise, a firing can be an excellent public-relations exercise, providing stimulation and relieving the tension of repressed hostilities. Your staff would rather believe you courageous than cowardly. They will respect and admire you for accepting the full burden of your responsibility as a leader. But if you dodge your duty, then you invite the sneaky suspicion that you are weak."

Timing the Firing Properly

Many feel that the best time to fire an employee is **late Friday afternoon** for the following reasons:

★ It provides an automatic **two-day cooling off period** for all involved.

★ **Other employees are busy** thinking about their plans for the weekend and are not as likely to be affected by any unpleasantness of the situation.

★ It gives the fired employee **time to clean out** his or her office immediately without the distracting presence of other workers.

★ If necessary, it **allows you to call a meeting** first thing Monday morning, when your employees are ready to start the week, to explain the firing.

[Note: There are also arguments for mid-week firings—a viewpoint not shared by this author.]

Procedures to Follow

Avert any potential problems by checking the company policy manual or employment letter. Written personnel policies and company handbooks can provide ammunition for a disgruntled employee.

Mark Watson, a Haddonfield, New Jersey attorney, tells of an employee who received money damages when his boss fired him with no explanation. "The employee manual said the company's policy was to discharge employees only for good reason and after conciliatory steps were taken. The company argued the manual was only a guideline. The court said it was evidence of a binding contract and the employee gave up other opportunities because of the statements in the manual," continued Watson. Know your policies and follow them.

If the person is at a high-level management position, there are other steps that may need to be taken. If the person has an employment contract, check with your company lawyer for prerequisites for dismissal and make sure you have the necessary grounds. Withdraw any signatory powers immediately and notify bankers, customers, and accountants that the person is no longer with the company and no longer has signatory powers. No additional explanation is necessary. Providing details may be seen as defensiveness on your part.

Have the employee turn over all keys, security cards, company material, and credit cards at the time of the firing. Don't accept the excuse that the employee needs to get a key or security card from home and will bring it by the office later. Occasionally a disgruntled former employee has used a key to get into the office immediately after being fired to purloin company material or destroy company property. If need be, tell the employee you will dispatch a courier to follow him or her home and pick up the missing items at once.

Make the Break Clean

Never act on impulse to fire an employee. But once you have thought out the action carefully and concluded that your company can no longer keep the employee, make the break clean.

Tell the employee that his or her services are no longer required, briefly state the reasoning that led to this decision, point out the warnings that were given previously, and emphasize that the decision is irrevocable.

Do not get into a long, involved discussion about the reasons for the firing at this point. Emotions are probably running high and an argument now will not benefit either you or the departing employee. Since being fired is a crushing experience, conduct the session with dignity. Any ego-boosting you can give, such as, "I believe that with your natural enthusiasm you'll soon find employment that is better suited to you," will be a kindness.

After collecting the necessary keys, credit cards, and company material, give the employee his or her final paycheck with all vacation pay and any severance pay included. Be sure all the money owed to the employee is included in this last paycheck. Don't skimp here as that may be cause for a lawsuit.

Thomas S. Hubbard, founder of the Thinc Consulting Group International, Inc., the first of the modern executive outplacement firms that have sprung up in the last 15 years, says, "Also include a list of benefits and options within those benefits, such as stock, insurance compensation, or pension bridging." Follow company policy to the letter.

Positive Aspects

It is important to remember that there can be positive aspects to a firing for you, the company, and the fired employee. Employees being fired are frequently relieved. It couldn't have been

215

pleasant for them to be under the stress of working in a bad situation. A researcher fired for a poor attitude confided that she had hated her job for years, but just didn't have the courage to quit. The firing gave her the kick she needed to make the career change she had wanted for quite some time.

You can point out that it is a new opportunity for the departing employee. If your company has an outplacement service, be sure to give the employee all the necessary information about such a service at the time of the firing. Firing an unproductive employee relieves you of an unpleasant situation and can be an opportunity for communication with the rest of your staff.

It depends on your management style, of course, but you could call a staff meeting for an opportunity to clear the air of any misconceptions that may have arisen and also as a training opportunity. Reemphasize company policies, point out unacceptable behavior, and reinforce good attitudes and behavior with praise.

DO NOT fall into the trap at this point of engaging in a discussion with the rest of the employees or allow them to put you in a defensive position. Simply give them the facts, reinforce the proper behavior, and end the meeting.

Checklist For Firing

All companies, regardless of size, should have a form to be filled out by the supervisor and signed by the fired employee at the termination interview. If your company does not have such a form, use the form on the next page as a starting point, adjusting it where necessary.

Additionally, the following checklist will serve as a refresher before the termination briefing:

- ☐ Was the employee **fairly and properly warned** about his or her work problems?
- ☐ Are the warnings and methods properly **documented**?
- ☐ Have you **timed the interview** to ensure that minimum distractions will occur?
- ☐ Have you **followed company policies** to the letter?
- ☐ Have your accounting and personnel departments **prepared** all necessary paychecks and outplacement information?
- ☐ Have you prepared to **keep the interview brief, dignified and on target**?

CHART 21

TERMINATION PROCEDURE

Employee Name _____ Title _____

Department _____ Location _____

Date of termination _____ Vacation due _____

Employee has received:

    Final paycheck   ____Yes ____No

    Vacation payment   ____Yes ____No

    Outplacement info.   ____Yes ____No

    Insurance info.   ____Yes ____No

Employer has received:

    Identification card   ____Yes ____No

    Bus. Travel card   ____Yes ____No

    Company credit card ____Yes ____No

    Keys   ____Yes ____No

    Parking permit   ____Yes ____No

    Office equipment   ____Yes ____No

    Other (specify)   _____

Other comments: _____

_____
Signature of employee

_____   _____
Supervisor's signature   Date/Time

Firing an employee is not easy, but delaying the action due to fear of its unpleasant aspects can hurt you, your company, and even the employee to be fired. Do it now and do it well!

CHAPTER THIRTY-SEVEN

HELPING THE BATTERED EMPLOYEE

A female employee calls up sick again. You, her boss, have had it; firing her seems justifiable. Look again. She may be the one out of every three women who are physically abused by a spouse or lover. The statistics are overwhelming. In the United States, women are abused every 18 seconds. A suburban housewife is just as likely to be abused as an inner-city woman.

Both women and men can be victims of batterers. This chapter will refer to females since they are more likely to be victims than males.

After reading this chapter you'll be able to answer the following questions:

- ☐ What **form** does battering and abuse take?
- ☐ What can you **do to help** the battered employee?
- ☐ Why is your **taking the situation seriously** of great importance to the employee?
- ☐ How can you **detect** signs of abuse?

Comes in Many Forms

The abuse takes many forms. It may be physical, emotional, or verbal. The abuser might punch, slap, kick, knife, or otherwise harm the woman; or he might threaten or harm the woman's children or relatives. An abusive partner will harass the woman at work, often showing up at her job in the hope that it will cause her to be fired. Then the woman would become more dependent on him, and he would be more in control of the relationship.

There are many types of abusers, all with excuses as to why they do what they do. There is the "Saturday night, I was drinking" abuser, the everyday assaulter who feels his wife is his property,

219

the once-a-month "I couldn't help myself" abuser, and the vengeful ex-husband or ex-boyfriend who swears "I'll never let you go." Usually the cause is deep-rooted. The abuser cannot tolerate himself so he acts out his anger on his intimate partner, accusing her of making his life unhappy.

At the Workplace

A troubled employee may appear depressed or show fatigue, weight loss or increased use of tranquilizers or stimulants. She may seem preoccupied, be unable to concentrate or even display irritability.

What can you do as supervisor to help an employee you suspect is being abused?

First, you can understand what abuse is, including the cycle of battering. According to Dr. Lenore Walker, there is a pattern to most violence.

In the first stage, the tension-building phase, a woman tries to behave according to her partner's wishes, to keep the children quiet and make a good dinner. Unfortunately, she cannot control the situation. Only the abuser can control the violence, although he always blames the victim, accusing her of provoking him.

The second stage, the actual battering, may last anywhere from one hour to several days.

The third stage is the calm after the storm. It is difficult for people to understand this "honeymoon" stage. Some abusers are sorry and behave almost like little children. Others are less conscience-stricken. While not overtly sorry, they are at least not actively wild. Usually the victim is grateful for this peace and hopes that it will continue. She may want to leave the abuser, but mindful of what that would mean—moving, changing the children's schools, job pressures, financial struggles, and family pressures from both her side and his—she stays. Therapist Joan Rabinor, L.C.S.W., points out also that the "security" of what is known, even if the woman is experiencing considerable abuse, is still preferable, often to the "unknown"—i.e. what will happen if she leaves.

Despite the victim's best efforts to keep her partner happy, the cycle of violence repeats itself. The tension builds up, actual abuse occurs, then for a short time there is peace.

The victim's job performance is naturally affected. At some point, she may admit to the problem she is having. At that point, as her boss, your responsibility is to take her seriously and to respect her fears.

Taking the Situation Seriously

Most abused women are afraid that they will not be taken seriously, that no one will believe them. Usually they tell their boss only after the partner's threats or acts of violence interfere with their performance at the workplace. The women no longer feel safe at work. Their partners may be phoning them at their job or visiting and making threats.

At a major bank in Connecticut, no one took one of the bank teller's fears seriously. She was afraid of her husband and claimed he was following, harassing, and assaulting her. Finally, he came to the bank and caused a scene that proved to be highly embarrassing for the bank manager, the employee, and the bank's customers. In such instances, it is not the employee who is the problem but the person who is assaulting her. Arrest may have to be an option.

The National Rural Electric Cooperatives Association reports that at one rural electric co-operative installation a husband made his way into the office and there shot and killed his wife.

Obviously, a place of employment is not a fortress. But there are steps that a supervisor can take to provide his or her employees with protection from intrusion on the job. At the very least, visitors can be screened. If an employee has asked that her husband be kept away from the workplace, her request should be respected. The husband may downplay the significance of the request, even charmingly laugh it off as a lover's quarrel, but his wife's concern should be taken seriously.

Detecting Abuse

An observant supervisor may detect signs of a problem. For instance, employees who receive but do not make a lot of phone calls may be suffering from harassment. Similarly, women with high absenteeism records may not be unreliable but may be victims of abuse. They may be waiting for visible injuries like black and blue marks or cuts to heal. They are ashamed of their situation and want to hide the evidence that shows their loved one beats them.

Also, supervisors should be on the look out for female employees who seem "accident-prone": women who often say, "I had a minor car accident," "I tripped over the kids toys," and so forth. They may be covering up the assaults on their body.

Some supervisors are hesitant to approach an employee they suspect is being abused. After all, it might seem to the individual that they are butting into her personal life. But these same bosses will fire the woman for high absenteeism, and that will certainly affect her life.

Positive Action

Without invading her privacy, it is possible to let an employee know that the company she works for is concerned. It's not inappropriate to discuss the woman's home life. As a supervisor, you might start off by telling the female employee, "I'd like to help you keep your job; you seem to be having some problems. You're usually a good worker. I'm wondering what's happening? Are there some personal problems interfering? Can I help in any way?"

If you suspect that one of your employees is being abused, or asks outright for your help, you can refer her to your local battered-women's service or domestic-violence service. A battered women's service will not pressure her to stay or leave the situation. Rather it will try to help her make sense of all the enormous pressures she is under. An abused women's service can give her legal advice and counseling, offer her support groups so that she can talk with other abused women, and help with child care, housing information, job development, and so forth. Most services offer hot-lines and counseling to help the woman break her cycle of silence.

You may encounter resistance from the employee. She may not be ready to do anything. That, perhaps, is the toughest part of helping someone, knowing when to step back. You can offer your help and let her know that when she is ready you will do what you can.

To find out about the domestic violence service in your area, you can call the emergency room of your local hospital or your police department's rape/crisis center.

Here's a checklist of what you can do to help a battered employee:

- ☐ take time to understand the problem
- ☐ take the employee seriously when you are called upon
- ☐ show your support by asking if you can help
- ☐ safeguard the workplace from intrusion

☐ refer your employee to appropriate counseling services.

This concludes Section V, "Tackling Problems Professionally." Section VI, "Handling Departing Employees," represents a shifting of gears. Chapters 38 through 41, examine the problems involved when a good employee wishes to depart.

SECTION VI

HANDLING THE DEPARTING EMPLOYEE

One of the many heartbreaks that a supervisor experiences over the years is the departure of a good employee. The phenomenon is increasing with each passing year. Ten years ago the average job turnover rate was in excess of four years. The job turnover rate nationwide is now under 3.7 years. Our society has long been termed highly mobile and despite record-high mortgage interest rates, mobility continues unabated.

Nevertheless, the fact that good employees depart frequently for greener pastures can be of little solace to the manager or supervisor in a small or highly specialized department who had come to rely on someone who consistently performed well.

Don't Take it Personally

It's important to remember that the departure of a good employee should not necessarily be taken personally. The employee is not so much leaving your department or your company as he/she is seeking greater opportunity, a new challenge (or as is often the case, the experience of being disappointed elsewhere).

It's a sad fact of contemporary society that the greatest increase in income that a worker can achieve is through a change in organizations rather than through an increase in compensation in one's present organization.

In the following chapters we'll look at:

- ☐ clues for detecting the job seeker
- ☐ tips for inducing an employee to stay
- ☐ preventative and maintenance procedures for the impact of future losses
- ☐ guidelines for parting company effectively and gracefully

CHAPTER THIRTY-EIGHT

DETECTING THE JOB SEEKER

Way back in Chapter Five you read about Walter Ross who was stunned when one of his employees, Al Morris, abruptly resigned from the company. We learned in that chapter of the existence of built-in-turn-over factors which, if present, increase the probability that new employees will turn over much too quickly.

This chapter focuses on employees with whom you may have been working for several months, if not years.

When a good employee on your staff is actively seeking a job elsewhere, invariably there are several significant clues present that will indicate to you what is happening long before the employee hands in the resignation slip. It is important to know when a good employee is hunting for a new job and to be able to recognize the clues offered.

This chapter will enable you to answer the following questions:

- ☐ Why is it valuable to **learn in advance** of a potential departing employee?
- ☐ What **changes in appearance** may be noticeable?
- ☐ Is it appropriate to **check up** on employees who report in sick?
- ☐ What **office behaviors** provide clues?
- ☐ What other **subtle clues** may betray the job seeker?

The Inside Score

The loss of a good employee's skills to your organization represents an economic setback; your skilled labor or talent supply has been reduced. However, there are other reasons, perhaps of less significance, but nevertheless of some importance to total operations. For example, a good employee (or a bad one for that matter) may seek a new job while being financed through you.

This does not imply that the employee is not doing the job, but that he or she may be "coasting" on a fine effort previously executed and, in fact, presently doing only the minimum job necessary.

Linda Neuhaus, benefits co-ordinator for a major petroleum company observes, "An employee's leaving for a presumed better job causes other employees to think that the grass may be greener elsewhere for them, too." The departing employee may later provide new employment contacts for remaining employees. Neuhaus says, "Good employees know who else is good and who is ripe to be plucked from the organization."

Often, an employee's efforts do not affect the total operations until a week, two weeks, or sometimes a few months later. Thus, it is easy for some employees to coast for a significant length of time before leaving the old job for a new one. What are the clues that will tip you off far in advance that a good employee is job hunting?

Change in Dress

A male employee who suddenly starts wearing three piece suits to work with a new overcoat, matching tie pin, expensive watch or other paraphernalia may be attending job interviews during lunch or getting up early in the morning and attending them before work, (if he is seeking employment in the same city) or may be leaving work at 4:30 or 5:00 p.m. to head across town for a job interview.

Whether or not the employee normally wears a three piece suit, or a suit at all, the important "tip off" is to look at the employee's shoes. Few good employees would ever enter a job interview with shoes that are unshined; however, many good employees often go to work each day with shoes that are unshined because they are secure in their present job and no one is really observing them critically each day.

If a female employee is job hunting, you may detect crispness in her hair style, shoes with a slight heal, and she may be carrying a brief case or some type of business folder that day, as opposed to the conventional hand bag. "The female job seeker," says Neuhaus, "seeks a slimmer, taller appearance." Women may also choose to wear "a business suit, perhaps with a color coordinated scarf or bow tie."

Unfortunately, many times when employees have job interviews, that is the day that they choose to call in sick, and thus no clues

226

are provided concerning their dress or appearance.

If it is suspected that an employee is job hunting rather than home sick, it might not be a bad policy to get in the habit of calling personally to wish the employee better health, or to learn they perhaps "just stepped out" at the moment you called. It's within an employer's right to call occasionally when an employee is sick, at the very least just to determine how the employee is feeling and when they think they might be coming back. This is not prying or playing "Big Brother" because the employee is probably being paid for the day. As long as they are being paid, you have a vested interest in assuring that they are not getting a free ride.

Increase in Clerical Activities

Have you ever detected that one of your employees has been mailing a number of envelopes, or seems to have some sort of preoccupation with clerical activities when, in fact, clerical activities are not part of the employee's job? This may be a tip off that they are job seeking. While most employees will mail resumes and do much of their "homework" of the job search at home, often it is more convenient to send a few letters during the lunch hour or to mail letters at a downtown mailbox so that they will be sent out faster.

Some employees may even begin to use the office typewriter and some of the plain typing stationary or plain white bond paper for their own purposes. It is very important to check the use of the office copier, as many job seeking employees will use the copier to maintain a record of letters sent, to copy job search expense receipts or to maintain a copy of other correspondence.

If you suspect that an employee is using office materials and appears to be more interested in some of the clerical activities, the best way to handle the situation is to approach the employee casually and ask the question: "Is that for the XYZ report, or are these the exhibits for the study on DEF?" When asking such a question you will automatically force the employee to offer some type of explanation as to what the materials in question are. It is a mistake to ask an employee **directly** what the materials are, because they may have mentally rehearsed what's going to be said if they are confronted with the clerical or office materials, and thus the answer will provide less information. Also, you may cause a confrontation. By using the recommended questions, the employee might be "scared" out of working on, or with, these materials any further. They may then realize that they have a job to do for you, and they may think that nothing else was on your mind when you posed the question.

Avoidance of Eye Contact

It's almost a universal phenomenon that when good employees who have worked for you and participated in some of the major successes of the company are undertaking a job search, it becomes very difficult for them to look you in the eye on a sustained basis. In fact, as they grow closer to the time in which they believe that they are leaving, they generally try to keep eye contact as brief as possible or avoid it entirely. Be aware of this phenomenon of eye contact avoidance, particularly at staff meetings, and during one to one discussions with the employee.

If you suspect that the lack of eye contact is due to the employee's desire to leave the firm, you might ask if something is troubling the employee because he or she "seems a little on edge." The typical response will be of this nature: "I just haven't been feeling like myself lately," or "I'm a little tired these days," or "Oh, I don't know." If the employee does in fact give an answer that is similar to one of these three responses, there is a high probability that something is "up." If they give a direct answer that sounds like an accurate reason and you still suspect that they may be job hunting, you will have to look for other clues.

Richard A. Connor, Jr., National Director of Marketing for Pannell, Kerr, Forster, one of the nation's largest accounting, tax, audit, and management advisory services firms, says that "one sure tip-off is when discussion of career goals elicits less than enthusiastic response." Connor recalls the case of one young, high potential tax accountant who (to his surprise) recently departed Pannell, Kerr, Forster. In retrospect, all the evidence is there. Connor says that glossover statements such as "we need to do more about that," or "gee, that's nice" often appear with regularity in the parlance of the job seeking employee.

An excellent way to determine if a recent avoidance of eye contact is an indication of a planned departure, is to ask the employee out to lunch. Once again, if they are planning to depart, then lunch should prove to be a bit uncomfortable and they may offer some resistance, or perhaps postpone it for a few days.

Subsequently, you **will** be taking the employee to lunch and it is important to sit across the table so that the employee has no place else to look but at you. You might then discuss some of your plans and projections for the coming year and ask the employee how he or she feels, and how they may best fit in.

A job seeking employee might have an extremely difficult time after such a question is posed and may refer to how the company may best achieve those plans, while not necessarily including themselves in the response. A typical response might be something that sounds like this: "Well, I think the department could be doing a, b, and c and then after six months proceed to d and e." Notice within that response there is no mention of what they personally might be doing, their level of participation, or anything at all that refers to themselves.

Increased Telephone Messages and Time on the Phone

If you walk past the receptionist's desk and notice on a continuing and daily basis, that an employee suspected of job hunting has an inordinate number of telephone messages, this is a clue that a job search may be under way. If, when passing the employee's desk or office you happen to look in for a second, and see the employee on the phone repeatedly, though this is not a regular part of the employee's task or responsibilities, this is a signal that the employee may, in fact, be contacting prospective employers.

This is a bad situation for two reasons; one, company time is being used to undertake the job search, and two, even if the job search is not being undertaken, for whatever reason, the employee is using your telephone to conduct business that is not necessarily in direct support of your company. Although it is necessary to allow employees to use the phone and conduct their lives in the manner in which they choose (as long as they do a good job at work and are consistent with company policy and procedures) it is nevertheless undesirable to observe an employee making inordinate use of the phone.

A harmless question that might disarm an employee and yet is effective is: "Is that G company calling about those shipments for Thursday?" or "If that is Mr. X, tell him about the meeting that has been moved up a few hours." Regardless of an employee's phone-usage level, if, for any reason, you denote that the quality or level of effort regarding the employee's tasks and responsibilities are falling, it is time to take the employee aside and ask if there are any personal problems or ask if there is anything that you can do to help. At no time should an employee be allowed to have free rein at the office solely because you suspect that he or she may be job hunting and you are afraid that anything you may do will hasten the departure.

This is a common problem among small business owners and managers at all levels, because very few of us have had training in termination or parting procedures.

Other Changes in Behavior

There are other minor, or less subtle changes in the employee's behavior that you may denote, that may indicate that he/she is contemplating leaving the firm. One mode of behavior is characterized by a slight cynicism regarding company goals or projects that are on-going or about to be undertaken. This cynicism will not usually be revealed at larger company meetings; however, it is more inclined to be revealed in small group settings, especially with co-workers and subordinates.

New-found personal organization or neatness traits are also an indication that something may be stirring. Often an employee will start dismantling his files and reference materials in advance of his or her departure. Also, very often employees will throw out obsolete or irrelevant files or information so as not to clutter their desk or drawers, and symbolically their minds.

Another subtle clue and one that is rather difficult to recognize is the employee's use or overuse of the medical/dental benefits provided by the company. In many instances, departing employees have decided to get that check-up that they have been meaning to have for some time. Some employees will also become acutely aware of the terms regarding the policies and fringe benefits so that they can obtain maximum value prior to their departure. Another minor clue is when an employee becomes acutely aware of the number of vacation days, sick days and company leave that have accumulated, and can be seen in conversation and consternation regarding exactly how much time has accrued.

It should be remembered, that these behaviors, as stated above, are only minor clues to some of the more major ones discussed previously, as **many** employees are acutely aware of their fringe benefits and often show great concern as to how much time or benefits have accrued to them. Nevertheless, a good employee who previously has not exhibited this behavior, who is presently doing so, may in fact be contemplating leaving the company.

Here's a checklist of items that may tip off a job seeking employee:

- [ ] change/improvement in **dress** and hairstyle
- [ ] increase in **sick days** used
- [ ] increase in **clerical-type activities** by non-clerical employees
- [ ] **avoidance** of eye contact
- [ ] increase in **phone messages** and usage
- [ ] display of mild **cynicism** or sarcasm regarding organization goals
- [ ] improvement in personal **organization**—desk, files, shelves
- [ ] interest in **fringe benefits**, amount of leave built up, etc.

In the following chapter, ways to possibly induce a departing employee to stay are discussed.

CHAPTER THIRTY-NINE

INDUCING A GOOD EMPLOYEE TO STAY

Kimberly Mathers was almost certain that her best staff member, Lisa Knight, was job seeking. All the clues were there, and worse, Lisa's pattern of absenteeism and reporting had shifted in the last months.

If you have detected several clues and feel very strongly that one of your employees is job hunting, and if you have a good rapport with the employee, take him or her aside and talk about it openly and honestly. It should be understood that we are all seeking to better ourselves and sometimes we have to leave a good position and a good company for a better opportunity elsewhere.

After reading this chapter you'll have a better understanding to answer these questions:

☐ **What can you** as supervisor **ask** of the job seeking employee?
☐ Is it appropriate and/or useful to make a **counter offer**?
☐ Is it OK **to counsel** employees that are planning to depart?
☐ Why is a **close encounter** valuable in getting at the real issues?

Seek Continued Performance

If you can converse with the employee regarding the job search, as Kimberly finally did with Lisa, there are certain fundamental requests as manager/supervisor that you can make. First, you can request that the employee steadfastly give 100% effort while continuing to be employed at your firm, and can look forward to increases in pay and promotions, if, while during the job search, their efforts merit such advances. You can also ask to be kept informed.

If an employee is presently speaking to several prospective employers but doesn't have a particular job in mind, there is nothing wrong in his or her telling you that he/she does not contemplate a move for at least another three to four months. This gives you much more information than if they contemplate leaving in thirty days, and allows you to counteract any job offer that the employee may receive.

With the Good Ones, Counter Offer

While it is not recommended for every employee, with some you may say, "Come to me when you think you have got your best offer and we will talk about how I may be able to help you match it here."

One owner/manager of an Oregon office supply distributorship offered this simple formula for retaining your best employees, "What ever they're offered at another company—match it! You'll both win in the long run." Obviously, this is not a policy to be broadcasted, but does warrant consideration. Presenting a counter offer allows you to talk to the employee at the time when they are perhaps at the height of indecision. If the offer that they claim they have received is much more than you care to match, you may then decide that it's not worth keeping them, at that price. However, if the offer is in line with what you may be willing to advance them to, retaining the **good employees** may yield a far greater cost savings than the replacements you would have to find.

There is no question that many employers take very good employees for granted, and unfortunately never do begin to appreciate them until they realize that they are going to lose (or after they've lost) the employee (See Chapter 29, "Undermining the Ideal Employee").

If your relationship with the employee is very well developed, you may even serve as a type of job counselor for them. After all, you hired them in the first place, you saw skills and abilities that you felt could be used in your company, and very often you know their strengths and weaknesses better than they do.

It is not uncommon for an employee to depart from a job for a year or two, only to return. They too often recognize that your organization wasn't so bad after all, or that there really were more opportunities for advancement with you than they had originally recognized. Or, perhaps, you have expanded your operation and they now visualize the ability to make a long term sustained contribution to the future success of the department.

Close Encounters

Periodically, sit down with employees on an individual basis and try to relate on a gut level. Relating at a gut level means asking an employee, for example, what's really on his or her mind, or "how could we really improve things," or any other type of question that elicits an emotional, deep-seated response. This type of encounter is excellent in developing a good working relationship—particularly with key employees—and for gaining more information relating to a key employee's quest to depart.

The point of this encounter is not to make the employee uneasy, but to try to prevent a good employee from leaving (if they are contemplating leaving and the situation is reversible). You may discover that the employee doesn't want to leave and may have some personal problems or frustrations with which you may be able to help. Don't write off or give up on the good employee—often the desire to jump ship passes.

Here's a checklist of what can be done to induce a departing employee to stay or to ensure that the parting is mutually comprehended:

- ☐ Request continued **high performance.**
- ☐ Ask to be kept **informed.**
- ☐ Try to get an **advanced** departure date.
- ☐ Explore making a **counter-offer.**
- ☐ Consider serving as **counselor** to the employee.
- ☐ Arrange a **close encounter.**
- ☐ **Don't give up** on the good employee.

In the next chapter we'll examine both before and after measures to reduce the impact of the loss of a key employee.

CHAPTER FORTY

REDUCING THE IMPACT OF LOSS

Mark Thurston knew that Jerry Willis was leaving as of the end of the month. Still, Mark spent no time finding a replacement or preparing for the disruption in work flow. Mark was too busy putting out the daily fires and was unrealistic in his approach to reducing the impact of the loss of Jerry, a key employee. Perhaps Mark thought "things would take care of themselves."

Act, Don't React

Many supervisors believe that preparing for the loss of a key employee requires a defensive, even reactive, management style. This is not so. The flow of labor throughout business is a dynamic process and while some employees are particularly adept in handling given tasks and responsibilities, the distinct possibility exists that **subordinates currently with the company** can more than adequately fill the shoes of the departed employee.

What steps does the prudent manager take to minimize the disruption in operations when a key employee departs?

When a good employee departs, especially if it was on the heels of another employee departing or if it was on short notice, a typical response of a supervisor is to panic. This panic may take the form of revisions in policy procedures, issuance of memorandums, or conversely, light enforcement of organizational procedure in dealing with existing employees in the weeks and months to follow. All of these reactions represent poor management.

The overriding conceptual framework from which the supervisor's action should be derived is that employee supervision is basically sound, good employees will always be seeking opportunities elsewhere, the majority of employees will continue in the same productive manner, and, most importantly, new, good employees can once again be identified and recruited.

235

One suburban Detroit accounting firm maintained a policy of honoring departing employees with a farewell luncheon. This did not accelerate their turnover rate and was a strong indication of the firm's relative strength and stability.

Rotating Applicant File

The creation of a rotating applicant file is a necessity even in the best of times. When you are fully staffed and everything is humming, the rotating applicant file must be maintained. What is a rotating applicant file? This is a file of job applicants whom you have recently interviewed and with whom you must maintain contact for at least a six to nine month period. In other words, the wise manager should always be interviewing to gauge the quality and availability of human resources outside of the organization. Proper maintenance of the rotating applicant file means that even in the face of a quick departure on the part of a key employee, you'll have several potential applicants with whom you are already familiar to call upon.

This is so important. Think back to the time you hired someone who either didn't accept the job at the last minute or departed after a few months. If you keep in touch with the more qualified applicants, you won't get caught short.

The easiest way to initiate the rotating applicant file is to establish a policy of continuous interviewing irrespective of immediate staffing needs. Then your staff will not be suspicious or anxious over the fact that for one or two hours every week you are conducting interviews.

Cross Training

In college, most of us had a major subject area and a minor subject area. Why not apply the same principle to the organization or corporate setting? For those employees who can handle the responsibility, schedule a few hours each week for employees to gain experience in other tasks or in other departments. The schedule could be devised such that no department suffers a loss in person-hours, and the types of tasks and responsibilities offered need not significantly reduce overall productivity.

In the long run, cross training will in fact increase productivity as a network of employee skills is developed which serves as counter-balance to the loss of any particular employee.

Vacation Substitutes

Closely related to the strategy of cross training is the use of vacation time of a key employee to test others in the position. For example, if it is known that Bill Andrews is departing at the end of October for a one-week vacation, plan to schedule one of your employees to take on some of Bill's tasks during that week. This process should be open and above board and explained in detail to the entire staff.

Take care to give the substitute assignments in which he or she can make a measurable impact during the substitution period and which will not cause the returning employee to undo or redo the same work. If handled properly, the use of vacation substitute can be of great benefit to all.

Sitting in on Progress Reports

Another strategy to strengthen your department and reduce the potential loss of a key employee is to periodically invite staff members from other departments or with other responsibilities to meetings that the outside staffer might not otherwise attend. A variation on this theme would be to have outside staffers review reports, files and activities of other departments.

Again, the key to effectively executing this technique is to make sure that all employees are aware that this is company policy, and to minimize potential disruptions in personal and corporate productivity.

Wind Up Contingencies

Another strategy for reducing the potential impact due to loss of a key employee requires only a simple exercise which can be done at your desk in a matter of minutes. On a blank piece of paper write at the top "What would I do if Terry Wright resigned today, effective end of the month?"

You can fill in the name of anyone in your department, but this exercise is particularly useful when doing so for key employees. Now, under that lead question, list all of the contingencies available or which might become available if the employee were to leave. The available options will vary widely from company to company and from department to department.

Some options may include placing an ad in the Sunday employment section, soliciting the talent of competitors, promoting from within, abolishing the position and reorganizing the department, calling upon applicants in the rotating applicant file, or soliciting the opinions and advice of upper management. The point of this exercise is to illustrate that (1) there are options available and (2) only a minimum of preparation is needed to reduce the impact when a key employee departs.

Here's the chapter checklist:

☐ Remember that it is the **nature of the workplace** for people to move on to new challenges and opportunities.

☐ **Act, don't react**. Remain calm and do nothing drastic.

☐ Establish a **rotating applicant file**.

☐ Provide or secure **cross training** for your staff whenever possible.

☐ Use **vacation substitutes** to facilitate cross training of employees.

☐ Encourage other supervisors to allow **staff to sit in** on meetings of other departments.

☐ **Speculate** what you'd do if a key employee departed suddenly. Making a list of contingencies.

Chapter 41 , the final one in this section, focuses on parting company effectively and gracefully.

CHAPTER FORTY-ONE
PARTING WITH GRACE

D-Day is coming at the end of the month. One of your most productive staff members has accepted a job elsewhere. You tried all of the suggestions in Chapter 39, and undertook all of the contingency planning suggested in Chapter 40. Is there anything else you should do before the final departure?

Yes.

If a good employee is leaving and you know it, and if the two of you have spoken and it is not possible to keep him or her from going, there are steps that can be taken to ensure that the parting is as professional and amicable as possible. Some supervisors use these final days to belittle, ignore or unfairly burden the departing employee, as if trying to get even. None of these behaviors is recommended.

Let's examine the steps that should be taken when you know that a good employee **is** departing, and help you to answer these questions:

- ☐ Why are letters of resignation, **nevertheless, useful** to obtain?
- ☐ Will a departing employee provide greater information at an **exit interview**?
- ☐ **When** should an exit interview be held?
- ☐ Do departing employees serve as **ambassadors** of you and your organization?
- ☐ Why is it important to **keep the door open**?

(Note: For a booklet containing all of this book's chapter-lead questions such as those presented above [over 200 in all!] and the accompanying answers, send $6.95 to Checklist, 3709 S. George Mason Drive, #315 E, Falls Church, VA 22041.)

Obtain Letter of Resignation

Requiring that a departing employee submit a letter of resignation is partially helpful in obtaining underlying causes for the departure. The "partially" is because many employees will chose to be diplomatic when putting anything down on paper that will become a part of their permanent record with the company. The resignation letter, nevertheless, is valuable because it may provide a relatively brief and focused review of the employee's situation.

Virtually all mid and upper-level management positions in business and industry carry an unwritten mandate which requires offering a written letter of resignation when departing. You are encouraged to obtain such a letter from **all** departing employees.

The resignation letter in itself represents an important exercise for the departing employee; perhaps he/she hasn't fully crystallized onto paper the reasons for the departure. The resignation letter also serves as a good starting point from which to begin the exit interview.

Exit Interview

Conduct an exit interview to determine precisely the reasons why each employee departs. Once a final decision to go is made, an employee will be more inclined to give you precise information about the reasons for leaving. This information is extremely valuable to you as supervisor because probably **no one** else **will ever provide** this type of **information while employed**.

It is important to remember that the departing employee is also an ambassador to, or of, your organization whether you wish them to be or not. At one time or another, they are going to be relating their experiences at your company with co-workers, relatives, friends, etc. Even if they had encountered several months of rough going for any particular reason, if the parting was amicable, they will be more inclined to speak favorably about the organization.

The exit interview should be held on the very last day, before an employee departs. The interview must be held in an atmosphere in which the employee and supervisor can calmly and quietly discuss the reasons for the departure. As noted, the resignation letter may not include all facets of the situation and the employee may relish the opportunity to present additional verbal commentary.

Many organizations use some type of exit interview form for the departing employee to fill out as part of the exit interview. See example, chart 22.

CHART 22

EXIT INTERVIEW

Please rate these statements according to your experience or opinion (5 = Best).

— You were delegated sufficient responsibility.
— Your work was praised and appreciated.
— There were enough promotional opportunities.
— Your job challenged you.
— You had the opportunity to use many of your abilities.
— You were encouraged to make suggestions or improvements.
— You felt free to make a complaint or grievance.
— You were supervised too closely.
— You understood the company benefit program.
— You were satisfied with the working conditions.
— You were given clear-cut directions.
— You understood how your work fitted with other work in the organization.
— You were asked to do too much.
— You felt underpaid for the work that you did.
— You generally knew where you stood and got sufficient feedback.
— Your supervisor was well organized.
— You received valuable on-the-job training.
— You disliked your job.
— You feel this is a good place to work

Please make any other comments on the reverse side.

If there is reasonable evidence that the departure was due to a soured relationship or friction with management, it is wise to remember that the delicate balance of personal chemistry between management and staff is dynamic in nature—ever changing and evolving. Also, the old adage "You can't please everyone" is especially true concerning employee relations. Employees seeking reasons to be discontent will always find them.

The exit interview should not be used as a last ditch effort by management to convince the employee to remain with the firm. Any tactics of this nature should have been attempted far in advance of the actual day of departure—one reason is that there is simply too much pressure on the employee on the last day to go ahead with the planned departure.

Even the world's best offer presented by management during the exit interview would be to no avail as management's integrity would be undermined in making such an offer.

Keep the Door Open

All of the points stressed in this and the previous three chapters lead to the notion that it is necessary to keep the door open—let the departing employee know that, for now, it is understood greater opportunity may lie elsewhere. However, things do change (and quite frequently in contemporary society) and, combined with the experience the departing employee will gain with other firms in other positions, and new opportunities that may arise with your company in the coming years, it may be highly desirable to reassess and rediscuss the situation one, two or three years hence.

An employee who is both good and smart will acknowledge the professional courtesy that you have provided in keeping the door open and in not too long a time may take you up on your offer.

There is one more fundamental reason to make the parting of good employees as pleasant as possible: they worked for you and they probably helped you to reach your goals, improve your department or make a profit, and while you may not have recognized it during the while, your relationship was prosperous.

Here's a checklist for a graceful parting:

- ☐ Do not **belittle, ignore or unfairly burden** a departing employee during remaining time on board.
- ☐ **Obtain a letter** of resignation.
- ☐ Conduct the **exit interview** on last day.
- ☐ Find a quiet, **calm setting**.
- ☐ Use an **exit interview form** to gain additional information.
- ☐ **Avoid trying to persuade** the employee to stay.
- ☐ Keep the door **open**.
- ☐ Reflect on the **prosperity** of the relationship.

Does it hurt to let the good ones go? Of course it does. Should the departure represent setback to you or the organization? No.

This concludes Section VI. In Section VII we'll examine a very important aspect of your career—managing it!

SECTION VII

MANAGING YOURSELF

Time was when faithfully executing the responsibilities of your job was all that seemed necessary to ensure that your career advanced at a rapid pace. This is not so today and in many ways has really never been so.

In order to succeed as a successful manager/supervisor in the 1980's and 1990's, you must realize that you must manage your career as vigorously as you do your staff. This section contains one large concluding chapter which examines how to facilitate career advancement strategies.

Though you may not consider yourself a salesperson, much of what you do on the job and certainly much of what would be needed in future positions requires developing persuasiveness and selling skills. The value of getting certified, breaking into print, joining with a mission and speaking to gain visibility are all also examined and help provide a blueprint by which you can outdistance the pack and increase your promotability. Note: my earlier book, *Marketing Your Consulting and Professional Services* (John Wiley & Sons) co-authored with Dick Connor, fully explores how professional services providers can effectively market their services and themselves, even if they are not "marketing" types.

Tips are also offered on researching your professional needs and mastering your professional reading which round out Section VII and provide you with the winning edge.

Maybe you have never considered career self-management as a necessary, useful and continuing responsibility. Hopefully after finishing this section you'll realize just how important it is and will have the necessary guidelines with which to begin.

244

CHAPTER FORTY-TWO

HONING YOUR PROFESSIONAL SKILLS

Honing your professional and interpersonal skills in the context of supervising for success entails face-to-face discussions with your staff, peer groups, boss and upper-level management.

In managing your own career, it is important to never lose sight of the notion that "selling"—communicating and persuading, and gaining exposure are valuable, almost mandatory skills for advancement.

This chapter will help you to answer the following questions:

- [ ] What is personal image?
- [ ] How can getting certified help your career?
- [ ] What are some of the advantages to getting an article published?
- [ ] Are there benefits in joining community associations?
- [ ] What are some key sources for researching information needs?
- [ ] Can you master that growing pile of reading material?

One key to a successful career is having a firm conviction of your own capabilities. This starts with a proper frame of mind. You may have superior supervisory and technical capabilities to offer, but this alone is not enough. Belief in yourself is transmitted to co-workers and associates above and beyond what you say. And as prolific business author Herman Holtz says, "If you don't believe in yourself, who else will?"

In Control and With Awareness

The manager/supervisor in control and with awareness knows each day and each week what he or she will be doing, and knows the same about the staff being supervised. This person takes the time to review strategies and approaches supervision in a controlled and effective manner. This type of professional knows that taking the time to maintain personal control maximizes presentation effectiveness and overall use of time.

Stephen W. Carey, Ph.D., CAE, executive vice president and chief executive officer of the Greater Washington Society of Association Executives represents one of the best examples I've seen of someone with supervisory management responsibilities who is fully in control of the responsibilities of his position. This control is reflected in the extraordinary effectiveness of his staff and in the vast array of services and activities provided by the Association.

The effective supervisor is eager to learn or read about new supervisory techniques. Also, he or she recognizes that the time invested in keeping the car tuned up, the office and files in shape, and the wardrobe spiffy, pays dividends. This person welcomes luck but doesn't count on it, knowing that a well-executed, sustained professional effort is the best road to promotion.

Your Personal Image

Image has been defined as the sum total of all of the perceptions others have about you and your capabilities. Every element of your job over which you have discretion will contribute to the development of an image. If that image is solidly developed and consistently displayed, the task of influencing your staff and upper management will be greatly enhanced. An excellent book on image is **First Impression, Best Impression** by Janet G. Elsea, Ph.D. For assistance with wardrobe and color coordination, consult Carole Jackson's **Color Me Beautiful** (for women) and **Color For Men.**

Your organization expects certain behaviors and characteristics of professionals in your field. Within this area of expectation, however, it is recommended that you develop your own unique image, for this is what will differentiate you from rivals. For example, the supervisor who has a black belt in karate, or who recently visited Europe, can cultivate a unique image based partially on the outside interests.

Here's a checklist for honing your selling professional skills:

- ☐ Remember, **everyone** lives by selling something.
- ☐ Have a **firm conviction** in your capabilities.
- ☐ Maintain personal **control** and awareness.
- ☐ **Cultivate** your personal image.

Getting Certified

Increasingly, professional certification is regarded as a necessary component of a successful professional career. The number and variety of certification programs available in all industries grows each year. When I first began as a management consultant in 1975, I looked forward to the day I could become a certified management consultant (CMC) by the Institute of Management Consultants. Happily, that day came on October 19, 1982.

Many professional societies allow you to use the designation "affiliate" while you are earning certification. Thus, as an affiliate, you can have the benefits of certification even before you complete the process. As a supervisor you can add to your professional credentials by seeking out and obtaining certifications that will enhance your reputation and standing in your organization.

Below are descriptions of three certification programs whose value will be immediately recognized by people in the field:

American Society of Mechanical Engineers(ASME)

Membership **is** certification for this group. The aims and objectives of ASME include producing creative solutions for technical, government, and society interface; encouraging personal and professional development, and fostering high ethical conduct.

American Society of Mechanical Engineers
345 East 47th Street
New York, NY 10017
(212) 705-7722

Certified Association Executives (CAE)

The American Society of Association Executives has developed a comprehensive certification program which focuses on all aspects of Association Management. Thousands have already been certified.

American Society of Association Executives
1575 Eye St., NW
Washington, DC 20005
(202) 626-2723

Certified Purchasing Manager (CPM)

National Association of Purchasing Management.This program is for purchasing and materials managers and encourages and recognizes continued purchasing education. American industry and government recognize the CPM.

National Association of Purchasing Management
496 Kinderkamack Road
Oradell, NJ 07649
(201)967-8585

Here are the names of three directories found in any library, that list thousands of professional, trade and technical associations and societies:

Gales Encyclopedia of Associations
Ayers Directory of Associations
National Trade and Professional Association directory (NTPA)

Find the group in your field and write to them to see if they have developed a certification program.

Breaking Into Print

You can enjoy a large number of benefits when you have an article printed in a business or professional publication.

The number of general, industrial, business, professional, and in-house publications has risen dramatically in the last fifteen years. by using **Bacon's Publicity Checker, Working Press of the Nation, Writer's Market, Ayer's Publication Directory,** or **Gebbie's All in One Directory**, you can obtain the name, address, telephone number, editorial content, fees paid, circulation, target audience and submission requirements for over 10,000 journals and magazines!

The primary benefits of getting published include the following:

☐ Establishing your professional credentials
☐ Creating a favorable impression
☐ Bolstering your self-marketing efforts
☐ Being invited to speak to groups.

248

The best topics for articles are derived from the successful **work that you have already done**. This may include reports, papers, summaries, guides and exhibits, etc., that you previously prepared which can be generalized and applied to a larger audience.

Here's a checklist of ideas for generating article topics:

- ☐ Make a list of job-related gripes and ways to redress the situation.
- ☐ Make a list of new developments in your profession.
- ☐ Start a clip file of articles that interest you.
- ☐ Make a list of 6, 8, or 10 ways to do something better.
- ☐ Recall your favorite professional experience, most unforgettable character, biggest disappointment, etc.

Speaking to Gain Visibility

If the mere thought of speaking before a group makes you quiver, then skip down to the next section. For you brave souls, many local organizations as well as civic and charitable associations actively seek speakers. Yet the program chair of these groups must often scramble to find an interesting speaker. As a volunteer speaker to local groups, you enjoy many benefits including: improving your presentation skills, enhancing your resume, gaining community and professional exposure and increasing personal confidence.

Your decision on whether to seek speaking engagements as a career advancement strategy hinges on your ability to be interesting and have something worthwhile to say to a group composed of selected targets. If you've never spoken before a group, you have a unique experience in store. Everyone is nervous at first, but in a little while you many find speaking quite exhilarating.

Joining With a Mission

How can joining outside groups help your career?

Earning a position of leadership in a high visibility organization is an excellent way to be of service and, as a by—product, enhance your career potential. By volunteering your services and assisting civic and charitable organizations, targets of opportunity (those that may provide your next job!) come to know you as a person and then feel comfortable in discussing their business problems with you.

Civic organizations such as the Chamber of Commerce, Scouts, and the YMCA afford business leaders and professionals ample opportunity to rub elbows with other key community and business leaders and jointly work on solving local, civic, public and business problems. When gaining personal exposure, it is assumed that you are fully competent in your profession and a rising star in the community.

Memberships in professional and civic groups should constantly be evaluated to determine if career advancing activities, in addition to personal satisfaction, is being realized. Otherwise, joining can be a drain on your time and energy.

For the supervisor on the rise, these groups offer you a chance to gain a measure of visibility that most of your peers and co-workers will never know.

Researching Your Professional Needs

As a supervisor, you undoubtedly recognize the need for timely research information. Obtaining information can be costly, either in human resources or dollars expended.

Here are some quick, relatively inexpensive ways to gather information.

Your public library maintains a copy of the **Business Periodicals Index**, **Reader's Guide to Periodical Literature**, and **Readers Guide to Scientific Literature**. Through these indices, you may scan for the latest articles on your industry, its customers or other topics.

Association directories can be found in any library and offer the names, addresses, and phone numbers of your industry's trade and professional associations. Three directories in particular, the aforementioned **Gales Encyclopedia of Associations, Ayers Directory of Associations,** and **The National Trade and Professional Association Directory (NTPA)** can provide trend information, surveys, publications, education programs, referral services, lobbying support, monthly newsletters and magazines, and many other services and activities.

If you need to research an article or information that appeared in your local newspaper, often your public library will contain a newspaper index that abstracts newspaper articles by topic and cross references this listing by date. The **Wall Street Journal Index**, for example, is available in many public libraries in major cities.

Here's a list of public library resources:

READERS GUIDE TO PERIODICAL LITERATURE
BUSINESS PERIODICALS INDEX
READERS GUIDE TO SCIENTIFIC LITERATURE
WHO'S WHO SERIES
ASSOCIATION DIRECTORIES
CARD CATALOG
NEWSPAPER INDEXES
Washington Post
New York Times
Wall Street Journal

MAGAZINE, MEDIA SOURCES
Working Press of the Nation

PUBLICATION SOURCES
Writers, Artists, Market
Bacons Publicity Checker
Literary Market Place
Standard Periodicals Directory
Gebbie's All in One

Federal Government Information Sources

The federal government is one of the largest publishers in the world. Through the **Bureau of the Census** Department of Commerce, you may obtain sales and revenue data on virtually any industry, by state, county, and standard metropolitan statistical area. To obtain a list of the bureau's publications, write to:

Public Information Office
Bureau of the Census
Department of Commerce
Washington, DC 20233
(202) 763–4051

The Department of Commerce also produces the **U.S. Industrial Outlook**, which traces the growth of 200 industries and provides five-year forecasts for each industry. The **U.S. Statistical Abstract** is a compilation of data and reports from the Department of Commerce, the Department of Labor, the Department of Transportation, the Small Business Administration, and other federal agencies.

Many of the major publications produced by the federal government are on sale at the U.S. Government Printing Office. For a free catalogue write to:

Superintendent of Documents
U.S. Government Printing Office
Washington, DC 20401
(202) 275-2051

Publishers and Information Services

Many publishers offer free catalogs listing numerous information directories that they publish. The Gale Press, for example, offers a directory of consultants and consulting organizations, a guide to research centers and even a directory of directories! Here is a sample listing:

MCGRAW-HILL
1221 Ave. of Americas
New York, NY 10020

NATIONAL RESEARCH BUREAU
310 S. Michigan Ave. #1150
Chicago, IL 60604

RUFF TIMES—TARGET PUBLISHERS
P.O. Box 2000
San Ramon, CA 94583

KLEIN AND SONS
P.O. Box 8503
Coral Springs, FL 33065

PREDICASTS
11001 Cedar Ave.
Cleveland, OH 44106

AMACOM
135 W. 50th St.
New York, NY 10020

Newsletters

Newsletters have become a valuable source of research information. Newsletters are now published by government agencies, industry groups, associations, political groups, virtually every type of group. The **Oxbridge Newsletter Directory** and the **Newsletter**

Yearbook Directory, list several thousand newsletters, arranged by functional area. The **National Trade and Professional Association Directory (NTPA)** indicates which of the thousands of associations listed maintain a newsletter. By accessing these directories and others your local librarian may suggest, you can gain access to late-breaking news and information of concern to you.

Befriend information sources such as librarians, publishers, and federal agency representatives, because you will often have the need to call on these people more than once.

Mastering Your Reading

If you're like most business professionals, the odds are you can't keep pace with all the information that passes your way and that may be necessary to absorb in pursuit of your supervisory efforts and towards the advancement of your career. In this "age of information," most business professionals are experiencing information overload.

Successful managers/supervisors of the 80's and 90's must be able to effectively supervise their staff, remain goal-oriented and yet stay attuned to the latest developments within the industry, advancing technology, and the field of management and supervision.

Active reading—seeking out those key publications and sources of information that supply you directly with what you need to know, is far more preferable than passive reading—reading those publications such as the daily paper, general interest periodicals and a variety of direct mail material you may receive which may take more time than they're worth.

If you didn't master skimming and scanning in high school or college, it's still not too late to learn. Skimming involves perusing the first one or two sentences of a paragraph within an article to see if the information within that paragraph is pertinent to your immediate quest.

Skimming can also be used when confronted with several journals or periodicals at the same time. The basic payoff to skimming is that it enables you to quickly determine whether or not you should invest any further time in the article or the publication at hand.

Scanning is a technique used with large volume materials. If you must research several books or periodicals for the purpose of extracting key information, scanning enables you to effectively handle the task in a short time. Scanning involves reviewing the table of contents, index, list of charts and exhibits, and occasional paragraph leads. The advent of high-speed photocopiers greatly facilitates the scanning process.

Reading at Your Desk

Suprisingly, may supervisors feel guilty about reading at the office desk. The guilt seems to stem from the fact that reading at the desk doesn't appear to be very productive and it certainly doesn't cause one to perspire. Many erroneously believe that if they're not in some form of motion then they're not really working or, worse than that, it appears to others that they're not really working. If this is a problem for you, you may wish to discuss the need to read at the desk with your boss and with your staff.

Reading Can Be Delegated!

Though you may not have considered it previously, a stack of periodicals you've been wanting to get through, those key chapters in the latest book, or those reports that have been piling up, don't have to be read by you at all. They can be delegated to any of your staff including the most junior.

All that's necessary to effectively delegate some of your reading workload is to provide clear instructions as to what you're looking for and how you want it to be presented.

The Data Bases are Here!

Better still is to subscribe to one or more of the various bibliographic data base services which quickly and conveniently afford you the ability to skim the contents of hundreds of current and dated periodicals across the broad spectrum of industries and professional disciplines. **Management Contents**, for example, provides a hard copy or terminal display of the table of contents of over 100 business and professional publications every two weeks, for a relatively nominal fee.

Management Contents
Find/SVP
500 Fifth Avenue
New York, NY 10110

Other on-line data bases such as Dialog and BRS provide an awesome array of information arranged by periodicals, subject, author and numerous other cross references. These services also provide virtually instant bibliographies for selected topics and yield informative, well-written article abstracts or, if so desired, entire article reprints (the fee for reprints is high, usually between $7–$12).

Here are the addresses and phone numbers of several leading bibliographic data base services and information sources:

COMPU SERVE INC.
500 Arlington Center Blvd.
Columbus, OH 43220

THE SOURCE
1616 Anderson Road
McLean, VA 22102

DIALOG
3460 Hillview Ave.
Palo Alto, CA 94304

BIBLIOGRAPHIC RETRIEVAL SERVICES
1200 Route 7
Latham, NY 12110

Book Review Services

Your reading time can also greatly be reduced by employing one or more of several excellent book review-type services. Sound View Executive Book Summaries, for example, capsulate leading management and business books into four to eight-page summaries and offer new titles every month.

Sound View Executive Book Summaries
100 Heights Road
Darien, CT 06820

Some of the leading business books are condensed in the pocket-size *Business Book Review*, which is published six times a year. From the hundreds of business books that are published yearly, the editors carefully screen to identify ten books for each issue.

Business Book Review
615 West Kirby Ave.
Champaign, IL 61820
(217) 398–2060

Another service is the **Wall Street Review of Books**, published by the Redgrave Publishing Company. This periodical is available quarterly for a very reasonable fee. For more information write to:

Wall Street Review of Books
Redgrave Publishing Company
380 Adams Street
Bedford Hills, NY 10507
(914) 241–7100

Why Not Listen and Learn?

You can greatly reduce your reading time by using your ears. Cassette services such as Nightengale-Conant, Newstrack Executive Tape service, and Listen and Learn greatly accelerate your information gathering capability.

For further information write or call the following:

Nightengale-Conant Corporation
7300 North Lehigh Ave.
Chicago, IL 60648
(800) 323–5552

Newstrack Executive Tape Service
Box 1178
Englewood, CO 80150
(800) 525–8389

Listen USA!
60 Arch Street
Greenwich, CT 06830
(203) 661–0101

Here's a quick review for mastering your reading:

☐ Redefine precisely what your reading needs are.
☐ Practice skimming and scanning.
☐ Read at a desk.
☐ Delegate reading assignments to your staff.
☐ Explore database services.
☐ Subscribe to book review and newsletter services.
☐ Reduce your reading time by using your ear—listening to cassettes.

Your Career in Perspective

Successfully managing your career involves time and effort and simply can't be left to the whims of fortune. The extra effort you put into advancing your career should be looked upon as a long-term investment.

The way to rise above the crowd is by not following it. Your two-pronged attack—successfully executing the responsibilities of your present position, and taking the extra steps to ensure your personal and professional development, should continue to be regarded as of equal importance. If you're willing to trust your instincts, carve your own path, and assume the risk of leadership, a spectacularly successful, rewarding career can be yours.

CHART 23
MAGAZINES & JOURNALS

**Administrative Management Society
(AMS)**
2360 Maryland Rd.
Willow Grove, PA 19090
(215) 659-4300

Association Management
Magazine of the American Society
of Association Executives
1575 Eye Street, N.W.
Washington, DC 20005
(202) 626-2722

Bureaucrat
Bureaucrat, Inc.
P.O. Box 347
Arlington, VA 22210
(202) 287-6070

Business Quarterly
University of Western Ontario
1393 Western Road
London, Ontario, N6A 5B9 CANADA
(519) 679-3222

California Management Review
University of California
Graduate School of Business
Administration
350 Barrows Hall
Berkeley, CA 94720
(415) 642-7159

Canadian Manager
Canadian Institute of Management
2175 Sheppard Ave. East #110
Willowdale, Ontario, M2J 1W8
CANADA
(416) 493-0155

Contract Management
6728 Old McLean Village Dr.
McLean, VA 22101
(703) 442-0137

Credit & Financial Management
National Association of Credit
Management
457 Park Avenue South
New York, NY 10016
(212) 578-4410

Human Resource Management
University of Michigan
Division of Management Education
Graduate School of Business
Administration
Ann Arbor, MI 48104
(313) 763-0121

Human Resource Planning
Human Resource Planning Society
Grand Central Station
P.O. Box 2553
New York, NY 10017
(617) 837-0630

Industrial Management
American Institute of Industrial
Engineers, Inc.
25 Technology Park/Atlanta
Norcross, GA 30092
(404) 449-0460

**Journal of Small Business
Management**
West Virginia University
Bureau of Business Research
Morgantown, WV 26505
(304) 293-0111

Journal of Systems Management
Association for Systems
Management
24587 Bagley Road
Cleveland, OH 41388

Manage
National Management Association
2210 Arbor Blvd.
Dayton, OH 45439
(513) 294-0421

Management Accounting
National Association of
Accountants
919 Third Avenue
New York, NY 10022
(212) 754-9747

Magazine of Bank Administration
Bank Administration Institute
60 Gould Center
2550 Golf Road
Rolling Meadows, IL 60008
(312) 228-6200

Management Review
American Management Association
135 W. 50th Street
New York, NY 10020
(212) 586-8100

Management World
AMS Building
Maryland Road
Willow Grove, PA 19090
(215) 659-4300

Personnel
American Management Association
135 West 50th St.
New York, NY 10020
(212) 586-8100

Personnel Administrator
American Society for Personnel
  Administration
30 Park Drive
Berea, OH 44017
(216) 826-4790

Personnal Journal
245 Fisher Avenue B-2
Costa Mesa, CA 92626
(714) 646-3931

Public Personnel Management
1850 K Street, NW
Washington, DC 20006
(202) 833-5860

Sloan Management Review
Massachusetts Institute of
  Technology
50 Memorial Drive
Cambridge, MA 02139
(617) 253-7170

Supervision
National Research Bureau
424 No. 3rd Street
Burlington, IA 52601
(319) 752-5415

Supervisory Management
American Management Association
135 West 50th Street
New York, NY 10020
(212) 586-8100

Training
Lakewood Publications, Inc.
731 Hennepin Avenue
Minneapolis, MN 55403
(612) 333-0417

Training & Development Journal
ASTD
600 Maryland Ave., SW Suite 305
Washington, DC 20024
(202) 484-2390

CHART 24

PROFESSIONAL SUPERVISORY AND MANAGEMENT ASSOCIATION AND SOCIETIES

- Academy of Hazard Control Management
- Academy of Management
- Academy of Product Safety Management
- Administrative Management Society
- American Academy of Ambulatory Nursing Administration
- American Academy of Health Administration
- American Ass'n of Industrial Management
- American Ass'n of Managing General Agents
- American College of Hospital Administrators
- American Management Associations
- American Soc. for Performance Improvement
- American Soc. for Public Administration
- Apartment Owners and Manager Ass'n of America
- Ass'n for Information and Image Management
- Ass'n for Management Excellence
- Ass'n for Systems Management
- Ass'n for Volunteer Administration
- Ass'n Field Service Managers
- Ass'n of Internal Management Consultants
- Ass'n of Management Analysts in State and Local Government
- Ass'n of Records Managers and Administrators
- Ass'n of Sales Administration Managers
- Ass'n of School Business Officials of the United States and Canada
- Audio-Visual Management Ass'n
- Automotive Trade Ass'n Managers
- Building Owners and Managers Ass'n International
- Business Forms Management Ass'n
- Club Managers Ass'n of America
- College Athletic Business Managers Ass'n
- Employment Management Ass'n
- Federal Managers Ass'n
- Financial Management Ass'n
- Healthcare Financial Management Ass'n
- Hospital Management Systems Soc.
- Hotel Sales and Marketing Ass'n International
- Institute of Ass'n Management Companies
- Institute of Certified Records Managers
- Institute of Management Consultants
- Institute of Management Sciences
- Institute of Real Estate Management
- International City Management Ass'n
- International Council for Small Business

- International Customer Service Ass'n
- International Facility Management Ass'n
- International Management Council
- International Material Management Soc.
- International Personnel Management Ass'n
- Life Office Management Ass'n
- Mail Systems Management Ass'n
- Medical Group Management Ass'n
- Nat'l Assistance Management Ass'n
- Nat'l Ass'n of Management/ Marketing Educators
- Nat'l Ass'n of Purchasing Management
- Nat'l Ass'n of Scientific Materials Managers
- Nat'l Ass'n of Service Managers
- Nat'l Contract Management Ass'n
- Nat'l Credit Union Management Ass'n
- Nat'l Institute of Management Counsellors
- Nat'l Management Ass'n
- Nat'l Safety Management Soc.
- Nat'l Soc. for Performance and Instruction
- Nat'l Soc. of Professional Resident Managers
- Office Technology Management Ass'n
- Product Development and Management Ass'n
- Professional Convention Management Ass'n
- Professional Managers Ass'n
- Project Management Insititute
- Property Management Ass'n of America
- Society for Advancement of Management
- Soc. for General Systems Research
- Soc. for Information Management

Further Reading

Books

Auger, B.Y.:**How to Run Better Business Meetings: An Executive's Guide to Meetings that Get Things Done**, 8th ed., 3M Company, St. Paul, MN, 1979.

Batten, J.D.: **Tough-Minded Management**, American Management Association, New York, NY, 1963.

Beach, Dale S.: **Personnel: The Management of People at Work**, 2nd ed., The Macmillan Co., New York, NY, 1970.

Blake, R.R. and J.S. Mouton: **Executive Achievement: Making it at the Job**, McGraw Hill, New York, NY, Nov. 1985.

Blanchard, Dr. Kenneth and Dr. Spencer Johnson: **The One—Minute Manager**, Berkeley Books, New York, NY, 1982.

Bliss, Edwin C.: **Getting Things Done: The ABCs of Time Management**, Charles Scribner Sons, New York, NY, 1976.

Boyan, Lee: **Successful Cold Call Selling**, AMACOM, New York, NY, 1983.

Bradford, Leland P.: **Making Meetings Work: A Guide for Leaders and Group Members,** University Associates, San Diego, CA, 1976.

Brown, Arnold and Edith Weiner: **Super Managing**, McGraw-Hill, New York, NY, 1985.

Carkhuff, Robert R.:**Sources of Human Productivity**, Human Resource Development Press, Amherst, MA, 1983.

Chambers, Carl D. and Richard D. Heckman: **Employee Drug Abuse: A Manager's Guide for Action,** Van Nostrand Reinhold, New York, NY, 1972.

Connor, Richard, A., Jr., and Jeffrey P. Davidson: **Marketing Your Consulting and Professional Services,** Wiley, New York, NY, 1985.

Crosby, Philip B.: **Quality Is Free,** New American Library, New York, NY, 1979.

Davis, Keith: **Human Relations at Work: The Dynamics of Organizational Behavior**, 3rd ed., McGraw-Hill Book Co., New York, NY, 1967.

Dobrish, Cecelia, Rick Wolff, and Brian Zevnik: **Hiring the Right Person for the Right Job**, Franklin Watts, New York, NY, 1984.

Drucker, Dr. Peter F.: **The Changing World of the Executive,** Times Books, New York, NY, 1982.

Dyer, Frederick C. and John Dyer: **The Enjoyment of Management,** Dow Jones-Irwin, Homewood, IL, 1972.

Elsea, Janet G., Ph.D.: **First Impression, Best Impression,** Simon & Schuster, New York, NY, 1986.

Finch, Frank: **Encyclopedia of Management Techniques,** Facts on File, Inc., New York, NY, 1985.

Garner, James E.: **Safety Training for the Supervisor,** Addison Wesley Publishing Company, Reading, MA, 1969.

Goodman, Stanley J.: **How to Manage a Turn Around,** The Free Press, New York, NY, 1982.

Groder, Martin G., M.D.: **Business Games: How to Recognize the Players and Deal With Them,** Boardroom Books, Millburn, NJ, 1980.

Hegarty, Edward J.: **How to Succeed in Company Politics,** McGraw-Hill, New York, NY, 1976.

Hon, David: **Meetings that Matter,** Wiley, New York, NY, 1980.

Jackson, Carole and Kalia Lulow: **Color For Men,** Ballantine, New York, NY, 1984.

Jackson, Carole: **Color Me Beautiful,** Ballantine, New York, NY, 1984.

Jewell, Mary B. and Diane L. Jewell: **Executive Style: Looking It . . . Living It,** New Century, Piscataway, NJ, 1983.

Joseph, Joel D.: **Employees' Rights in Plain English,** National Press, Bethesda, MD, 1985.

Kanter, Rosabeth Moss: **Change Masters,** Simon and Schuster, New York, NY, 1983.

Kerzner, Harold: **Project Management for Executives,** Van Nostrand Reinhold, New York, NY, 1981.

Killian, Ray A.: **Managers Must Lead!** AMACOM, New York, NY, 1982.

LeBoeuf, Michael: **The Greatest Management Principles in the World,** Putnam, New York, NY, 1985.

LeBoeuf, Michael: **Working Smart,** McGraw-Hill, New York, NY, 1980.

Likert, Rensis: **The Human Organization: Its Management and Value,** McGraw-Hill Book Co., New York, NY, 1967.

Lunborg, Louis B.: **The Art of Being an Executive**, Free Press, New York, NY, 1984.

Lusson, Michelle: **Creative Wellness**, Warner Books, New York, NY, 1986.

Marstellar, William A.: **Creative Management**, Crain Books, Chicago, IL, 1985.

MacKenzie, Alec R.: **The Time Trap—Managing Your Way Out**, McGraw-Hill, New York, NY, 1975.

McCormack, Mark: **What They Don't Teach You at Harvard Business School**, Bantam, New York, NY, 1984.

McDonald, James O.: **Management Without Tears**, Crain Books, Chicago, IL, 1981.

Mintzberg, Dr. Henry: **The Nature of Managerial Work**, Harper and Row, New York, NY, 1977.

Morrissey, George L.: **Management by Objectives and Results**, Addison-Wesley, Reading, MA, 1970.

Peters, Thomas J. and Robert H. Waterman: **In Search of Excellence: Lessons from America's Best Run Companies**, Harper & Row, New York, NY, 1982.

Renton, Michael: **Getting Better Results From the Meetings You Run**, Research Press, Champaign, IL, 1980.

Rosenberg, Gail, S., ed.: **Alternative Work Schedule Directory**, First Edition, National Council for Alternative Work Patterns, Burlington, VT, 1980.

Snell, Frank: **How to Hold a Better Meeting**, Cornerstone Library, New York, NY, 1976.

Strauss, George, and Leonard R. Sayles: **Personnel: The Human Problems of Management**, 3rd ed., Prentice-Hall, Englewood Cliffs, NJ, 1972.

Tannenbaum, R., I. Weschler, and F. Massarek: **Leadership and Organization**, McGraw-Hill, New York, NY, 1961.

Toffler, Alvin: **The Third Wave**, Morrow, New York, NY, 1980.

Uris, Auren: **The Executive Deskbook**, Van Nostrand Reinhold Company, New York, NY, 1970.

Von Oech, Roger: **A Whack on the Side of the Head**, Warner Books, New York, NY, 1983.

Vroom, Victor H.: **Work and Motivation**, John Wiley and Sons, New York, NY, 1964.

Yoder, Dale: **Personnel Management and Industrial Relations**, 6th ed., Prentice-Hall, Englewood Cliffs, NJ, 1970.

Glossary

Battered Employee—in the work place, a battered spouse who has been abused physically, emotionally or verbally, including being punched, slapped, kicked, knifed, or otherwise harmed.

Brainstorming—posing a question or problem to a group and recording without qualification any suggestions, recommendations made as quickly as they are expressed.

Blind Box Advertisement—a classified ad soliciting employment inquiries and/or resumes that doesn't identify the advertiser.

Built-in Turnover—factors present in a hiring situation that increase the likelihood of early departure on the part of a new employee.

Calendar Blockback—a method of achieving goals by starting from the due date or deadline for a project and working back towards the present to establish interim deadlines or milestones.

Certification—a formal program, offered by an accredited association or professional society signifying the education, experience, competence, and integrity of the awardee.

Credentials—awards, achievements, certification, and experience signifying one's professional standing in a chosen field of endeavor.

Cross-training—providing employees with experience or exposure to new tasks, or other tasks in other departments which are not a part of their normal responsibilities.

Cycles of Productivity—the internal time grid followed by productive employees that enables them to handle certain tasks and assignments as their energy level dictates, such that they consistently achieve optimal results.

Data Base—focused information compiled and arranged for easy access and flexible use.

Delegation—assigning responsibility to others for specific tasks.

De-motivation—factors that lead to reduction in enthusiasm, initiative or output on the part of your staff as a result of something you've done.

Employee Turned Institution—an employee who has effectively ceased functioning in the role or position for which he or she was originally hired and actually contributes very little to the job.

Exit Interview—a formally scheduled meeting between you and a staff member on their day of departure which addressed why he or she is leaving.

Exposure—gaining visibility and insights and experience beyond one's immediate working environment, i.e. throughout the entire organization, the community, or the industry.

Flex-time—an alternative work schedule which capitulates to the needs of employees for whom regular 9 to 5 hours are not desirable.

Job Description—a written summary of the key components of the tasks, duties, responsibilities, and experiences a candidate should have to successfully handle a given position.

"Ideal" Employee—someone who comes to work on time, willingly puts in over-time, always gives one-hundred percent, is loyal and a definite asset to his or her organization.

Image—the sum total of all of the perceptions others have about you and your capabilities.

Listening—the process of actively engaging in what is being said by another to you.

Manager—one who "tells people in fairly specific terms what to accomplish and then counsels them to the extent necessary in their efforts to accomplish these objectives."

Milestones—interim steps towards pursuit of a goal or a project deadline.

Motivation—factors within each individual which cause him or her to act.

Moonlighting on the Job—any secondary income activity that one engages in while on their regular full-time job.

Objectives—established goals or desired end results, often quantified.

Orientation Checklist—an established system, usually on a pre-printed form, for fully acquainting and acclimating a new employee to his or her new position and organizational environment.

Paternalistic Supervision—a form of management which condescends to employees, i.e. not keeping them informed of both good and bad developments affecting the organization.

Probation (On Probation)—a trial period of the act of granting continued employment of an existing employee on the promise of improved behavior.

Probationary Period—a predetermined amount of time in which a new employee is evaluated to determine if he or she will be permanently retained.

Productivity—systematic efforts to "increase, extend or achieve

human and organizational benefit outputs and decrease resource inputs."

Push Policy—a technique for combatting chronic absenteeism
which includes a verbal message, a written notice, and, if
necessary, suspension/discharge.

Question Funnel—an interviewing technique which involves
beginning with broad, relevant questions, working towards
the specific.

Ready, Fire, Aim—the concept of making a brief evaluation or
assessment of a task at hand, followed by undertaking of the
task at hand even if on a piecemeal or limited basis, followed
by readjustment or modification of activities if necessary.

Rotating Applicant File—an ongoing, updated compendium of
resumes of professionals who have the skills and capabilities
needed in your organization but who may not necessarily be
needed at the moment.

Scanning—a reading technique used with large-volume materials
involving reviewing table of contents, index, lists of charts
and exhibits, and occasional paragraph leads.

Skimming—a reading technique involving perusing the first
couple sentences and paragraph within an article or chapter
to see if the information is pertinent to your immediate
quest.

Supervisor—someone who "oversees one generally cohesive function and specifically tells people what to do and how to do
it, while also maintaining many of his or her own operating
duties."

Termination—the formal process of firing an employee in strict
accordance with your organization's policies and procedures.

Under-achiever—one who's productivity is not commensurate
with his or her experience and capabilities.

Would-be Lou Grant—a boss who thinks he or she is tough but
fair, but in reality is only tough.

AUTHOR'S BIBLIOGRAPHY

"Developing A Team Atmosphere" by Jeffrey P. Davidson, CMC. **Successful Woman**, July/August 1985, Volume 7, Number 1.

"Speeding Your Professional Reading" by Jeffrey P. Davidson, CMC, **Computer Decisions**, July 30, 1985, Volume 17, No. 15.

"When You Have To Face The Problem Employee" by Jeffrey P. Davidson, CMC, **Office Systems 85**. June 1985, Volume 2, Number 6.

"Giving and Receiving Criticism" by Jeffrey P. Davidson, CMC, **Supervisory Management**, May 1985.

"When Employees Know The Bad News It Can Be Good For The Company" by Jeffrey P. Davidson, CMC, **Office Systems 85**, April 1985, Volume 2, Number 4.

"Stop On-The-Spot Hiring, And Check Applicant References" by Jeffrey P. Davidson, CMC, **Convenience Store News**, March/April 1985.

"The Year Ahead" by Jeffrey P. Davidson, CMC, **Publishing Trade**, January/February 1985, Volume 4, Number 1.

"Learning to Listen" by Jeffrey P. Davidson, CMC, **Successful Meetings**, September 1984.

"How to Tell If You're a Bad Boss" by Jeffrey P. Davidson, CMC, **Tools of the Trade**, New Jersey Bell, June 1984.

"Time-Saving Tips for Conducting Research" by Jeffrey P. Davidson, CMC, **Phoenix Business Journal**, Volume 4, No. 23, April 16, 1984.

"Paper Tigers Come in More Resumes Than One" by Jeffrey P. Davidson, CMC, **ABA Banking Journal**, April 1984.

"Making Friday Afternoons More Productive" by Jeffrey P. Davidson, CMC, **Successful Woman**, March 1984.

"Planning for the Loss of a Key Employee" by Jeffrey P. Davidson, CMC, **Canadian Manager**, Canadiana Institute of Management, Ontario Canada, April/May/June 1984, Volume 9, No. 2.

"Ah, Those Innocent Late Afternoon Assignments" by Jeffrey P. Davidson, CMC, **Cincinnati Bell Magazine**, Vol. 74, No. 6, December 15, 1983.

"A Mini Thesaurus for Business Writers" by Jeffrey P. Davidson, CMC, **Supervisory Management**, December 1983.

"Controlling Staff Turnover" by Jeffrey P. Davidson, CMC, **Today's Office**, August 1983.

"Managing Cycles of Productivity" by Jeffrey P. Davidson, CMC, **The Rotarian**, Vol. 143, No. 2, August 1983.

"Five Common Mistakes Managers Make After Achieving Moderate Success" by Jeffrey P. Davidson, CMC, **Manage**, of the National Management Association, July 1983.

"New Creatures in the Office Jungle" by Jeffrey P. Davidson, CMC, **Supervisory Management**, July 1983.

"Don't Manage Out of the Office" by Jeffrey P. Davidson, CMC, **Toastmaster**, Volume 47, No. 12, December 1981.

"Eight Ways Even an Ideal Employee Can Run Into Trouble in the Job" by Jeffrey P. Davidson, CMC, **Management Quarterly**, NRECA, Vol. 22, No. 3, Fall 1981.

"Beware of the Employee Turned Institution" by Jeffrey P. Davidson, CMC, **The Commercial Record**, Volume XCIX, August 21, 1981, No. 34.

"Communication Company Objectives" by Jeffrey P. Davidson, CMC, **Personnel Journal**, April 1981.

"How to Tell When a Good Employee is Job Hunting" by Jeffrey P. Davidson, CMC, **Supervision** Vol. XLIII, No. 2, Feb. 1981.

"Favorite Employee Timewasters" by Jeffrey P. Davidson, CMC, **Management**, U.S. Office of Personnel Management, Washington, DC, Volume II, No. 1, Winter 1981.

"In Praise of Portable Dictation Equipment" by Jeffrey P. Davidson, CMC, **The Office**, Volume 92, No. 5, November 1980.

"Self Protection For Business" by Jeffrey P. Davidson, CMC, **Boardroom Reports**, Vol. 2, No.1, January 15, 1977.

"Ten Tips on Survival for Small Business" by Jeffrey P. Davidson, CMC, **New Englander**, Vol. 23, No.6, October, 1976.

INDEX